WHAT WE LOVE WILL SAVE US

# What We Love Will Save Us

## Essays

DAVID OATES

Kelson Books    Portland

Published by Kelson Books

For information please write to: kelsonbooks@gmail.com or

Kelson Books
2033 SE Lincoln
Portland OR 97214

Front cover photograph and author photograph
by Horatio Hung-Yan Law

Book and cover design by Steve Connell / Transgraphic Services

The text of this book is set in Stempel Garamond, a 1924 version
of types designed by sixteenth-century printer Claude Garamond,
who based his designs on late-fifteenth-century Venetian typefaces.

*Printed in the USA*

ISBN 978-0-615-31419-8

# Acknowledgments

I owe thanks to many for material help, invisible encouragement, and thoughtful critiques.

To my friends, thanks for lifting my spirit in good food and drink and laughter. To Horatio Law, more thanks than I can put into words for your shaping insights which helped me find the path for this book.

Special thanks to manuscript readers Tim Chapman, Jeff Gersh, Mary Elizabeth Braun, and Claire Sykes. For advice on selected essays and on the project as a whole, many thanks to Ana Maria Spagna; and thanks to fellow Wild Writers Sara Cartmel, Dot Hearn, and David Pickering.

Thanks to individuals and institutions providing me time and space for this work: to Clark College for granting a sabbatical; to the Spring Creek Project of Oregon State University, for writing days at Shotpouch Creek in the Coast Range. And gratitude for a month as Writer in Residence in highrises along Portland's downtown river through the South Waterfront Artist-in-Residence program.

Ana Maria Spagna and Laurie Thompson gave me lodging and support during high water writing times in the North Cascades. Doug and Trish Woodward generously provided time at a cabin on the Stehekin River. No plumbing. Rushing waters. Perfect quiet.

And thanks to Abeille Kaelin in Taos, New Mexico for good spirit and desert spaces in which to review the project in late stages.

I am thankful for events where essays were read and listened to and developed: "The Other Portland Symposium," organized by Rhoda London (February 2007); Oregon Press Women's Association (May 2008); and ASLE Association for Literature and Environment (Victoria, B.C. June 2009).

Some of these essays appeared in the Portland *Oregonian*; *ISLE* Interdisciplinary Studies in Literature and Environment; *High Country News*; and *Oregon Land* (American Society of Landscape Architects); or were syndicated through *Writers on the Range*; or appeared in the anthology *Portland Queer*, edited by Ariel Gore.

Special thanks to *High Country News* editors Michelle Nijhuis and Jodi Peterson, who have often welcomed my work.

Lastly, and (almost) without irony: To editors too many to mention who rejected manuscripts, or ignored them, or offered good advice, or bad advice; who failed even to correctly register the genre, or held them for months then didn't read them, or responded sincerely, or sent little xeroxed rejection slips; and who in general steadily demanded more edge, more heart, more velocity, more relevancy, more delight: Thank you.

# Table of Contents

## I. UNLOCKING

August 2003    *What We Love Will Save Us* . . . . .    11

*On Pleasure* . . . . . . . . . . . .    15

*Six Good Places* . . . . . . . . . .    19

*Empty Pods and Pleasant Graveyards* .    29

*Poetry on the Elliptical* . . . . . . .    33

December 2007    *Forgiving the Present* . . . . . . . .    37

*Imagine* . . . . . . . . . . . . .    51

*Unlocking the Hips* . . . . . . . .    55

*Banner Peak* . . . . . . . . . . .    61

*Un-hating the Muir Trail* . . . . . .    65

*Things I Have Experienced
    but Do Not Believe In* . . . . .    73

February 2008    *Red Door* . . . . . . . . . . . .    77


## II. RENDERING

January-May 2007    *Rendition* . . . . . . . . . . . . .    85

*After Rendition . . . Silence* . . . . . .    99

*And after Silence?* . . . . . . . . .    109

*Lacking the Subjunctive* . . . . . . . 113

*Threat Level: TEAL* . . . . . . . . 121

*The Real Fake* . . . . . . . . . . 125

*When Denial is Public Policy* . . . . . 137

May 2008     *O Felix Obama* . . . . . . . . . 141

*How To Be a Progressive
(Without Believing in Progress)* . . 149

*City Gods and Sacred Waters* . . . . 153

*I Am Already Dead* . . . . . . . . 167

August 2008     *Under Pressure We Make Lists* . . . . 173

November 2008     *Epilogue: Night Thoughts and Music,
Three Days before Election* . . . 179

Notes    . . . . . . . . . . . . . 183

# I. UNLOCKING

# What We Love Will Save Us

AUGUST 2003

It's a hundred and four in Sacramento and almost that in the gold-rush foothills where my folks live, whom I've come six hundred miles, dutifully, to visit. But I've settled into the duffy shade of a huge mountain hemlock, the sweat of a perfect dayhike is cooling me, and a snow cornice gleams above a silver-dollar lake set deep in its talused cirque.

I love this. The High Sierra.

I loved it in detail, over years of exploring, before I abandoned the sins and automotive savageries of California for the cool green urbanisms of Portland.

In my hand is a book of poetry – Stephen Dunn's – and I'm about to enter a long, savoring poem listing his "Loves." In detail. Things and people and . . . how much he loves! And with what precision and determination: The ocean in winter. Shifting from second to third.

> I love the carpenter bees
> in spring, mating in air, and I don't mind
> the holes they make in my house . . .
> I love the way sorrow and lust

can be companions. I love the logic
of oxymorons, and how paradox helps us
not to feel insane.

I guess it's a kind of epicure's trick, to save a book like this
for a moment like this. But it works for me, helps lift me
from the pettiness of my familial disapprovals and frictions.
You know what I mean: the morbid power a loved one's
ill-concealed faults can exert over you. In my family (as in
yours, I bet) there is racism and fundamentalism and bigotry
– smug, impervious to evidence, infuriating. I'm the gay son
come home to make nice for a few days. Each night I call my
partner – whose name is never uttered here – to try and draw
strength from the thin stream of voice in the earpiece.

I hiked up here today across glacier-slick granite a-dance
with streams and melts and trickles under that famous sharp
and somehow divinizing light. Pines limber and lodgepole
are gardened into it, a bonsai wide as the world, with tiniest
greens of grass and flower lipping the pools and tumbles. I
loved this, and I came here to love it again. But instead, for
half the journey, I have been rehearsing the unspoken argu-
ments that muddy up my heart: making the iron-clad *q.e.d.*
for global warming (yes it's real!), for diversity and inclu-
sion, for a bigger god . . .

We are all, too much of the time, captives of the wreck
and the mistake. Can't take our eyes off it, can't stop thinking
about it, can't stop picking that scab. We slide into our merely
negative identity – defined by what we refuse.

But it's not enough, is it. Is our nation adrift, hijacked by
mountebanks and neocons and thugs? It is not enough to

hate them. We must remember what we love. Time spent saying *no* is, at some point, time robbed from the *yes* that must follow. A long time ago I read Jesus' words "Do not resist evil" and wondered what in the world he could have meant. Maybe this: We must stand on what we love – live it, be it and bring it. And not waste time in the other direction, preaching up devil and denunciation. In mere reaction we become impotent and diminished – as I know well. It's no place to live.

Tired but refreshed, I return toward evening and find a meal set specially for me, of pork chops seethed in sweet apples and onions. A hundred-dollar-bill is tucked in at my place, to help with the trip. So wrong on the macro, on the micro these are good and loving folks. What can I do but love them back?

There's a random dangerous rightness abroad in this wide shining world. It's a rightness, not a correctness. We don't need so much to counter other people's errors as to bring the light and joy of that right and beautiful world: what we desire for our planet and ourselves. What we are doing instead of hating and denying and bombing.

If I live to be my parents' age I'll have three more decades to help Portland develop its answers: how we'll live in a warming world without cheap oil. Will it be a good life in 2033? Every day, in my adopted hometown, we struggle and argue, build and make choices toward a *yes* – one that might someday be useful all over our swaggering, sweltering, beloved land.

Our job is to work on what we love. Daily. In detail. With precision and determination.

# On Pleasure

What is this sweet brain feeling?

If I walk early on a September morning, before the moneymaking day has broken in upon us. If the sidewalk seem a path that goes back further than I can remember. If movement be blessing, movement itself, the motion of muscles, the filling of lungs, the release of air. And if the head swivel to take in foreground and middleground, then lean back suddenly beneath trunk-and-branch space, that opening-up feeling like a leafy brain. The sky behind it large with color before daybreak. How shall I assess the pleasure, where is it pleasuring, what parts are headbound, how much down in the ropy red brainspine, how far out into the threads of selving, follicles, tips, touches?

Pleasure is the most elemental fact of life and the one we may forget soonest. Forgetting, it turns into a problem, gnawing experience mindlessly, turning pleasure into consuming, one ecstatic bite of cinnamon bun becoming a useless loaf of it, a pre-turd merely.

The problem, Puritans, is not pleasure. The problem is forgetting it.

\* \* \*

But only pleasure, never connoisseurship.

How to explain in mere words what speaks to the whole body? There's a love duet at the heart of that silly opera *Der Rosenkavalier* – when it lifts and modulates and resolves upward and then upward, one darker soprano and one lighter, flying together like Blake's morning larks, tip-tip, or like halves of a double helix carrying million-year codes into the deep, far galaxy of desire and the commitment of one soul to another that is the single most extraordinary event in the universe.

That singing is what a kiss is like with my beloved – who like me is a man on the downward slope from fifty, our charms abating. No matter. Our kiss echoes that song. Or does that song really echo our kiss? I couldn't say. They are prismed together, one shading off into the other. All real pleasures are without hierarchy, I guess. Each one absolute. And more sacred than a dozen decalogues of prohibition.

A sip of red wine carries me nearly as far. Now, there's a whole overdone lingo about wine, practically operatic, which I ignore. No doubt I possess an unworthy palate. Yet certain odors and aromas do take me up, even before my lip is wetted – twitches are delivered and perhaps for a moment a hound-dog's ecstatic sensorium is experienced at whatever my lowly hominid capacity is. I do respond, that I am sure of. A lot. The red wine winking under my nose sends off rose petal. Citrus. Honey. Smoke. And delight, don't know how else to say it. Why smells should make me so tickled is, well, that's the topic. What is tickle, except being alive?

And then the tongue gets involved, tip tip, sides, back, playing and awakening and revising and reporting this particular rainbow and palette and river-of-savor that juices over the teeth and into the happy happenstance of a mouth. Well let's say it's a zin. I live in Pinot noir country but my plebe heart sings to a zinfandel, which is sturdy and has an oaklike trunk of tannin that will pucker a few seconds into the swallow and give some structure to the basket of summer fruit you might luckily have slurped at first swipe. So, to review – first there's this aroma and then sweet juicy and then this stand-up-straight square-shouldered militancy, and your mouth is thinking now, isn't it? All kinds of intelligence being assessed down there and my isn't your brain along for a nice ride. The structure being framed is described as *briary*, jargon I actually like – which means something pointy and assertive, as if pepper or clove had been hidden inside the blackberry jam and served – yum – on a spoon of well-smoked applewood a bit rough-grained to the tongue. Like that.

But let's say it's a *good* zin and the ride is not yet over. After you've been stood to attention, your back-tongue and that soft dome of pleasure above it will melt, will suggest, will sublime a whole gentle pantheon of lingers. Shadows of flavors escaping language will flicker, like soft-shifting sun-dapple, oak boughs, spring day . . . Zither. Estuary. Plumb-bob. You pick the words, I can't find any and I admit it – I'm grateful to be in a zone where writing and thinking can't follow, a darker cave, interior, alive.

※ ※ ※

Intoxication is officially a sin but it has been very, very good to me. This goes beyond sampling of course and so diverges my theme. Don't care. There were years when I was so overcontrolled that the tiny release in a pitcher of beer (at Everybody's Pizza, across the street from the graduate school) was practically necessary and deeply welcome. Once a week, I'd forego "closing the library" – grinding in my book-strewn carrel until lockup at eleven-thirty, then heading home for sleep and arising for more of the same, dour, ambitious, lonely. Though I had no head for liquor and was thin as a whippet, once a week I got a pitcher for myself at first (my buddy got one too, for his own reasons) because I needed that much just to unwind to some normal pitch of humanity. Then we'd share another. *This can't be good* I'd reflect. Yet it was the only technique within my reach. So I reached it.

And I would not call back one drunken minute. They were a mercy to me. Friendliness and bonhomie entered, that were barred all the rest of the week. I think I would not have survived without them.

Intoxication is a universal human desire. It too is both a pleasure and a need, sometimes even a sacrament. Wine at the feast-of-drinking-God's-blood, the Eucharist: tipsy, spirituous, open to the cosmos perhaps, tipping over into what bigger world than the language-laden one of daily trudging? That world the body inhabits, cave-dark and full of mysteries.

No doubt I've got vices but those seven deadlies have been seven livelies for me, avenues of fleshly living, incarnation. Eating. Drinking. Sometimes lucky, slippery, lickerous sex. Even Jesus had a body for a while, and my bet is, he enjoyed it.

As I aspire to.

# Six Good Places

There's a workaday village – or its ruins, anyway – hidden in the wilderness of the Sierra Nevada. I found it by following a feeling. It's a feeling mapped onto my brain by ancient forces. Lately this map has begun guiding me in other places: Venice. Vancouver. Aix-en-Provence. Seattle. Even Portland, where I live. And it has been telling me something crucial about how we ought to be building our lives in the coming urban century.

The map works like this. I was in the southern Sierras, walking along a lesser fork of the Kern River. Wide sagebrush valleys, sandy and hot, led me upwards towards cooler elevations, and eventually I began considering where to camp. I'd been making solitary explorations in mountains for many years and my mind knew precisely what it liked: big trees behind, maybe on steeper slopes going up to cliff so my back would feel covered. Campsite elevated a little, on open ground sloping down to a stream or lake. Views off that way and that way, as if to watch for danger or for dinner. Some rocks to sit on, flat and duffy between. That's what I wanted, and when found it brought a satisfaction I had learned to notice, in fact to *heed* because if the place was wrong then the night would be long and restless, I would feel morose and ill-fated and be eager to leave. But when it was right . . .

I sat a moment with my feet resting in open sagebrush but my back in the tall trees, the creek mumbling a few paces off. *Ah.*

＊ ＊ ＊

But soon I discovered that my mental map of a good place, so precise and demanding, was not my own at all: Obsidian chips like a glittering city lay scattered all over the sandy soil. Unknowingly I had come to make my camp amidst broken arrowheads, chips, middens everywhere. Suddenly I felt like a man in a crowd of invisible strangers. But not strangers, really – they had known this was *a good place* in exactly the same way I had: by following the inner map. I looked up and saw the smoke-blackened boulder, the ancient fire-ring. All afternoon, I walked directly to their best places, found their reminders. In something like a trance, I let my larger mind, the one that includes the body, make the decisions. It knew right where to go. Uncanny.

Later I discovered these people had called themselves "Tubatulabal." They lived there for a thousand years.

Time after time, in remote untrailed places, I have found my feet carrying me unerringly to the cold, rain-washed hearths of other sojourners, a few years old or centuries old. They are invariably in places that embody that same exacting inner/outer template. It seems we know what we like, and when we find it, we find each other there too.

❅ ❅ ❅

This inner map is the source of wisdom increasingly needed by our species. Because we are now building cities not villages, and they are making a huge demand on the planet. Some 75 percent of the developed world now lives in cities; and in the developing world, according to a UN report, a majority of the population will be urbanized by 2020. This is how we're going to be living for quite a while. We had better get it right.

It's an ecological imperative as well as a hominid one. For a while now environmental thinkers have been pushing us to revise our green disdain for cities. If we are to avoid over-running every wild field and rural acre with flaccid semi-civilized sprawl, we must make good, compact, pleasing cities. Places we really like being in.

And what I'm noticing is this: The places I gravitate towards in urban environs are not so different from those *good places* I find in the mountains. Take those hours I enjoyed in Vancouver, B.C. a week ago. There I was in the window seat, Granville Island Public Market, with my chin on my hand as I gazed and read. False Creek sparkled before me, alive in sun and quick-cloud-shade. On its other side, downtown residential towers rose like greenglass cliffs. In the foreground, passing crowds strolled just beyond the window with dogs and prams and half-heard laughter, rivery and alive themselves.

I like this public privacy. I seek it out wherever I go and even at home, repairing to some urban plaza where, without having to speak or be known, I can observe the passing spectacle. When it feels right, it offers just what makes those mountain sites appealing: some sheltering topography, a clear line of sight, a little water, and a certain sense of habitable proportion.

We're living in an era of urban renaissance and, especially out here in the West, I think this may be one reason: We've begun looking past our mythic, open-spaces individualism, and finding each other in good public space. We're rediscovering sociable pleasures that older civilizations have long known about.

Six months ago, for instance, I found myself settling into the oddly-shaped *Place des tanneurs* in Aix-en-Provence, that somehow works equally well as human habitat though it could hardly be more unlike that spot in B. C. I'm no Christopher Alexander (the genius of *A Pattern Language*), but here's what I noticed.

First of all is its scale. Just-rightness in habitat requires spaces fitted to the human body, spaces cozy and expansive in just the right ways. On that day in Provence, I strolled into the *Place* and saw a Moroccan proprietor bringing out his two small tables, for the hot sun had just angled low enough to shade his tiny shop. Both tables filled instantly.

I sipped. People local and exotic, old and young, entered the plaza, visited the record shop, the minute grocery, the eateries of many qualities, the hip graphic-novel shop called *Le bateau livre.* A quiet human stir, as of a breeze in the canopy. They liked it there. So did I.

The triangular plaza was not huge: I stepped off its base at just thirteen paces. The plaza itself was elevated by three steps up from the walk-street thoroughfare. Four-story structures enclosed it, faced in that Provence sandstone of buttery yellow, the upper residences opened by painted shutters and windows. In the midst, a great plane tree, and beside it a fountain of humane dimensions, cool and sittable. I measured it with armstretch, giving the cool grey stone a brief hug: six feet to a segment. The shape of a fountain – what's it mean?

It means that, if scale matters, so does design. A bit more majesty for that fountain would destroy its fitting-in-ness and my pleasure. A few feet of roofline the wrong way would cost that proprietor hours of trade.

For a contrast – which yet proves the larger point – you could swing by San Jose, California's "urban village" of Santana Row, where some five or eight brand-new blocks look strikingly like Aix: quaintly shuttered condos rising (too high) over almost-walkstreets, with tree-sheltered cafes and even a purloined bit of pointy gothic stonework by a fountain. Here the simple pleasures of sitting and strolling together draw citizens from all over the automobile-dominated wasteland of Silicon Valley – despite the fact that it seems really like Aix corporatized: Aix passed through spreadsheets, inflated to 150 percent, and denatured with a kind of Disney/EPCOT design process. Even so – people come. We're famished for this.

※ ※ ※

There's a language for this sort of thing. Geographer and historian Jay Appleton, writing in 1975, defined the essential qualities as *prospect* and *refuge*. He observed our attraction to certain edge-of-the-wood settings and offered an evolutionary explanation: the ecotone is good for us poorly-defended omnivores, who want to see but not be seen. Reading Appleton I had that unmistakable feeling of confirmation: shelter, view, water, topography. The human habitat.

You could criticize this explanation – many have – for its essentialist tendencies, for ignoring the ways experience and culture reshape the inherited peoplemind. But for me, the explanation still works as a rough template. We may translate cliffs into buildings, waterways into artificial ponds, and potential game animals into passers-by with shopping bags. But the habitats we gravitate toward are surely a reflection of our animal nature, in some considerable degree. With ecologist/anthropologist Paul Shepard, I'll hold that we are, at root, evolved beings whose past informs our present social and emotional needs.

So I'm happy with "prospect and refuge" as good serviceable concepts. But to complete the transition to urban places, I find I need to add a term. The best refuges and prospects in the world won't help an urban place that has no life. We say it without knowing quite what we mean – "oh, it feels so dead there." What's missing?

Process.

In natural settings, process is always present. Time passes visibly, in decay and death and rebirth, falling trees and rockslides, moons and seasons. When we stare contemplatively at river or shore, as often as not we're noticing this passage of time (water its ancient symbol) and the poignancy of our own fluid and temporary lives. In town, however, we may miss it, especially in the shinier bits of the New West which have obliterated all evidence of the past and with it, all sense of the temporal. But home is a *now* as well as a *here*. Process is time made visible, and the best urban places find a way to moor us – safely but vividly – in the stream of change.

I was thinking about this in an unassuming *campo* behind Venice's renaissance jewelbox church Santa Maria dei Miracoli, earlier this year. I took in the diminutive arching bridge, the three- and four-story houses fronting the square, the lone cafe. Lingered of course over the narrow one-boat canal, its water higher today than yesterday, the sun dancing on it and on puddles of backed-up seawater still standing in the courtyard from the overnight tide.

Venice itself is the most humane place I've ever been, and in that *campo* moment I realized how the presence of tidal water infuses vitality into the place – a freshening vigor stronger than the stupefying presence of a million tourists and tourist shops, able to wash away the corruption of Venetian politics and sweeten even the stink of history. There it was: process. No town in the world feels the natural pulse more immediately than Venice. And among this city's many assets – Mediterranean light, a thousand years of history and architecture, good plazas and good food waiting everywhere – nothing keeps it *alive* like the mere sea, this immemorial ebb and flow looping nature and culture together as they should be (and truly are).

That's what I want for the cities of my home range: something not static in our midst, a living process. I wonder if it might even lead us to the other virtues of scale and design, prospect and refuge. Some towns in the West are energetically rediscovering their riverfronts: San Antonio; Portland; even L.A. is planning to unlock its river. And yet to some extent the need for motion can be answered even without an ocean or stream to play with. In Aix I enjoyed the semi-natural process of pedestrian circulation, the parade of all ages imparting a sense of movement and transaction, perhaps even offering reflection on age and time. Maybe this is another way to understand urban guru Jane Jacobs' insistence on a bustling street life. There is time and movement in peoplewatching.

In our brand-new Western towns, a lively sense of time and process-unfolding is the element hardest to come by. We need to think about it more intentionally. Where there is a tide or a river – even a dry one – there is an opportunity to engage our place in *its* place. Where there is weather, there is opportunity. In Portland and Seattle you can find many fine new places to linger in. The ones that have a river or that look across at the Olympic Range do pretty well. Some that open onto street life are surprisingly fine too. Bigness isn't necessary, though a keen sense of proportion is.

In Seattle, try a window-seat at the French Bakery across from Pike Street Market, or the PACCAR Pavilion that lets you overlook the new Olympic Sculpture Garden, with Elliot Bay in the offing. See if you don't think these places are sheltered-and-prospected pretty nicely, with a vivid sense of the dynamic world. In Portland, come to the Keller Fountain and experience a secluded cosmos, scaled right and connected profoundly to water. Or ponder why the industrial-leftover patio space next to the giant brick smokestack in the Brewery Blocks satisfies as it does. A fine mystery to consider with a draft pint.

* * *

Hanging out in public may seem a trivial focus for thinking about what makes a good life. But let's not underestimate the importance of what sociologists have called "the third place" – an available human gathering that is neither home nor work.

Good public places actually encourage us to remember our connectedness and thus foster that most urbane phenomenon, democracy. For such places embody "the public realm" – a crucial space (both actual and virtual) where we meet ourselves and experience the puzzle of our separate and shared identities. Here citizens speak and the public good is hammered out. It's no fluke that coffee-houses in New York, Philadelphia, and Boston fomented our famous Boston Tea Party and its private-property-destroying, government-defying mischief.

Yet many Americans today seem to have lost the feel for being citizens as well as consumers. The public realm tends to disappear in our corporate-consumerist environment, which always wants to isolate people into individual units of consumption and fast turnover. But the *agora* of ancient Athens, birthplace of democracy, was both forum and marketplace (as well as hangout, legislature, and university). Our public urban spaces can be too.

That invisible company I kept creekside in the Sierras formed the starting point for my own journey back to town – where the natural good place becomes a natural *public* space, a shared space reminding us that we sit on the banks of rivers no one owns – rivers of generations and tides and currents. In answering our private habitat-yearning, good places also anchor us back to our other, larger self of fellow humans. People sitting just over there, strangers, laughing and talking together.

# Empty Pods and Pleasant Graveyards

Back in the 1960s when I was a Los Angeles kid, LAX airport planned a big remodel. Regional bigwigs envisioned a futuristic structure of some kind at the heart of it, so architects went on a Jetsons jag and ended up suspending a gleaming streamlined pod on two sweeping steel parabolas. It would be the theme building for the whole airport, with a theme restaurant.

So what did they name it? "The Theme Building." Apparently none of the leadership geniuses understood that "theme building" was a *category*, not a name. So it stuck. I see it every time I go back. It contains, of course, "The Theme Restaurant."

"So, what do you feel like eating tonight? Mexican? Chinese?"

"How about Theme?"

❖ ❖ ❖

Real-estaters seem gifted with this special form of cluelessness. They are, I think, the prophets of our time.

Greater Portland, where I live now, is the mecca of New Urbanism, that planner's utopia of a compact downtown ringed by a growth boundary and outlying town centers of mid-rise shopping and housing. Today Portland wears around its shoulders a necklace of these bustling civic neighborhoods, named "Tanasbourne" or "Orenco Station."

Out in east-county Gresham, though, the civic neighborhood has been named . . . "The Civic Neighborhood." Article included: *The*. For distinction. Am I the only one who thinks this is funny?

Poverty of imagination should never surprise us. Excellence is rare, I always remind myself – mediocrity (by definition) the norm. But there's a particular form of babbittry in real-estate-world that seems, well, exceptionally mediocre. Gresham should be proud.

By now I ought to be inured to the PR mentality that produces this kind of thing, that mind divorced from any reality except the commercial one. Money out, money in – what else exists, really? I remember well those treeless, waterless miles of bulldozed Los Angeles suburb baking under the semitropical sun, named "Lake Forest" or "WillowDale" or some such emptiness. No one notices the actual blazing desiccation, apparently. People buy, builders get rich. Vacuous pseudo-named pseudo-places are everywhere now.

Words divorced from meaning. Places divorced from locale. Isn't this the modern condition? Erasure of history and topography, and (therefore) of meaning. All of us afloat in strange denatured space: TV. Mall. Air-conditioned car. Suburb. Each of us in a sealed pod, separated, advertised-to, amused.

"But what's it *mean?* What's it *for*?" Language is how we navigate such questions, finding or making the meanings we live by. What will be left us if *Forest* means cul-de-sac, *Clean* (as in "clean air act") means a measurement of profitable dirtiness, *God* a political lever someone else pulls? If the words go empty, so do we.

Our response to this diet of nullity ought to be, not those vacant talk-show emotions of anger and blame, but hunger. Hunger. "O taste and see," say the scriptures. We ought to be ravenous for real *Forest*, thirsty for *River* not channellized (L.A.) or poisoned (Portland), crystal-clear about what's *Clean* or *unClean*, and famished for a *God* at least as big as the night sky . . . or the human heart. We need to eat, touch, taste this natural and invisible world – and never be satisfied with less. Certainly not with additional helpings of *Theme*.

✳ ✳ ✳

I know of Gresham-adjacent housing available for purchase in a place called Pleasant Valley. Or, for aspirations that run higher, in Happy Valley. The houses are huge, identical, crammed-in, horrifying. What's your problem, writer?

Suburbia is an irony-free zone. So, apparently, is America. We do not notice or question the mismatch between word and reality. We smile and we buy. Reality is whatever the slogan says it is. Candidates are sold this way. Houses are. Wars are.

I know a graveyard right next door to Happy Valley called – believe it – Pleasant Valley Cemetery.

Sounds great! Let's go!

# Poetry on the Elliptical

Hey, isn't this the opposite of poetry-mind? Here I am doing two things at once, chugging away on the Elliptical Trainer with Li-Young Lee propped up next to my water bottle. I have to move him to read out my caloric burn and strides-per-minute, while the digital timer remains visible below, metering out my life in crimson minutes and seconds. Blink. Blink. I'm going for forty minutes today and if I read poetry through the first twenty then I won't notice the dullness, the *proverbial* dullness of this treadmill business. Busy-ness.

"One thing at a time" I tell my writing students: *Try it – give up the ear-bud the constant music the text-messaging cellphone chatter doing two three four things at once. Stop. Breathe. Be present. Write from that still place, that undistracted center.*

But here I am on the hamster-wheel and distracting myself by doing something else. The still center would be the wheel's, not mine. Clearly I am Not Deep. Once a very spiritual person in Taos (where else) asked me – "Have you done any *work?*" – where "work" with that little backspin meant something like, oh, Gurdjieff, Rolfing, crystals, Edgar Cayce, meditation . . . anything elevated and, above all, non-mainstream (Hippy Gnostic, I call it: there's a secret to the universe and they've got it).

I answered "No," with that bland unrevealing smile I've perfected from years in the classroom. *Me? Work?*

No doubt poetry ought to be read in undistracted solitude, the clean opposite of poetry on the Elliptical. Yet two days later I'm at it again. Joanna Klink this time. And at about eight minutes, I find myself thinking (instead of reading her hard poems): Hey – isn't poetry itself really a play of opposites – *the synthesis of hyacinths and biscuits*, as Sandburg said? That's a good mantra while upping the pace, by the way. *Hyacinths. Biscuits. Hyacinths. Biscuits.* Puff puff. I wonder if other people's minds are like this, weird and busy and obsessive. I think Sandburg meant that, like all the arts, poetry incarnates the invisible. Spirit enfleshed in curious vehicles. Poetry is a neverending paradox because *we* are. I reel myself back in and read:

> It was enough to hollow us out
> The evenings left grasses half-wild at our feet . . .
>
> As for a long while we stood in a hall full of exits
> Listening for a landscape beyond us

Right there on the page, something limitless. Feel it.

Dickinson's famous definition – poetry is when you feel the top of your head come off. That's the infinite dome, the three-D, somewhere in the vasty spaces between words. Between the printed letters even. But when you squint – the way my freshmen do – looking for Meaning somewhere beneath, deeper, profounder – it can't be found. Because poetry's depth is on the surface. It's a water-strider, a soap bubble. If you break the surface, the game's over. The letting-it-happen space: a mind present at all points and no particular point. That's the float.

Reading Joanna Klink is like hearing jazz where the melody is implied, riffed, played all around but never stated directly. Hard poems require the reader to infer, to leap in imagination, to *aha* the missing. It's what freshmen hate about poems: "Why don't these poets just *say* it?!?!?"

Well, because there's pleasure in letting the mind go limber, following, catching the drift. Letting it play. And because life isn't easy and – so far – in my experience – never actually states what it's really about. We're inferring constantly, aren't we? (Though priests and gurus will, for a price, offer canned readings, confidently inferring the daylights out of every single bit of your life. They'd prefer you not wonder whether these are *your* answers – the implied center of *your* life's wacky constellation.)

Twenty minutes. Surrounded by equal fools I am glad to get the exercise. The pedals go around and forward and back around, impact-free oval pathways resisting gently if I tell them to. Yet for decades how I scorned the treadmillers! Such ratty racing, I would think as I ran by (*ran*, not jogged), collecting my longlegged mileage. *After months of thirty-mile weeks, a top-twelve finish in that big 10K. Six point two miles, just right for me. Ok, it was just the thirty-to-forty year old bracket. Still: that last mile, Santa Monica street closed for the race, mild downhill putting wings on . . . but the pounding in the knees, those unreliable knees . . .*

Gliding down from the hard part of my workout now I'm looking up, avoiding my avoidance. Poetry too demanding, so *Jeopardy* on the TV screens. Or that fit young man in the next row, and his very sheer nylon trunks. How strange this constant fleeing, from my books and scribbles I escape to the gym for a workout, the blessed body, but then that pushes me away and I climb into a poem rather than attending the grunt and sweat, then the poem's too hard too and I escape it as well. Typical.

An ellipse is an orbital path with two centers. An ellipse is also something left out. *Ellipsis*. How many centers has a life? Too many pulls and pushes. There we are in our wobbling orbits, trying to find the impossible solution. If I traced the trajectories of all my desires and aversions, would they sketch the edges of this missing thing? The void, the center implied like in jazz, but never stated?

I tell my Intro to Poetry students, with a little smile, that "Poetry effs the ineffable" – puts words to that which is beyond direct expression. What they don't know is that my smile is partly an inner imp that whispers – "Yeah, and f---s the inf---able." My spiritual side is sadly wound up with carnality. Fucking the infuckable. Or trying to.

Oh the big picture. Sometimes you get a kind of field-awareness, that float that's all points at once and a pattern seems seeable, though (so far) it doesn't *stay* seen. We're forced to smallify our attention constantly, as if life were nothing but Cratchits and ledgers, stuck in point-awareness. Wishing for the big space. Out there somewhere. In there somewhere. Forty minutes. I'm done.

# Forgiving the Present (in Three Tries)

DECEMBER 2007

*1. Yelling at the TV*

Here we are in the murk of the present. It's like the fog of war, except that the war is over there and the fog is here. Here in America we're unable to find our way, frustrated, baulked, angry, guilty. Yelling at the TV.

That's the image: yelling at the TV. Futile outburst aimed at government shills selling transparent falsehoods. At reporters who nod and curtsey. At an opposition that dithers and backs down.

It makes us all crazy, yelling at the TV. It makes me craziest of all, and I have to go on long walks to calm myself. I acknowledge I have no philosophical coolness to draw on, I am hot and wounded and I overreact.

But I am not alone. What is this sense of unreality that hangs in the air, this "am I going crazy" desperation behind the eyes of citizens? What is happening here?

\* \* \*

I understood in a burst of dread when our famously snarling Vice President unleashed a fresh propaganda offensive a few months ago. He proclaimed a thing so obviously untrue it made you mistrust your ears. Yet there it was, on the news, in the papers, dribbling out of the spokesperson's mouth. In the big picture it's a small thing, "a footnote in history" as the cliché has it (so I will indeed just footnote it\*). But what does it mean when your leaders dare you to disbelieve a self-evident lie?

At a minimum it means that their contempt for the public is complete. That normal standards of intellectual decency and the decorum of shared truth are abandoned. You remember it, perhaps – that respect for public discourse which appears in the Declaration of Independence: *A decent Respect to the Opinions of Mankind* demanded reasoning and evidence, which the Founders provided in eloquent detail. This was not propaganda. It was debate, conducted among equals. It believed that a kind of truth could be found and held in common.

This kind of truth is a shared asset, an aspect of the public

---

\* According to the Congressional Committee on Oversight and Government Reform (June 21, 2007): "The Oversight Committee has learned that over the objections of the National Archives, Vice President Cheney exempted his office from the presidential order that establishes government-wide procedures for safeguarding classified national security information. The Vice President asserts that his office is not an 'entity within the executive branch.'"

Vice President Cheney upheld this position for some months with a straight face.

realm. When I say "truth" I mean it in the lower-case sense: the shared reality we can piece together with reasonable diligence from pretty-good evidence. It is a thing of immense communal value – a thing we leave out in public, you might say – where it is easily traduced, stolen, vandalized (the paradox of democracy).

*Leave it alone!* we want to shout, but the vandalism continues and, like frightened homeowners, we begin drawing the blinds of our national house, peeking out fearfully at the travesty.

✻ ✻ ✻

So when, a few months later, the sitting President's chief and most famous former advisor began tearing up huge chunks of known reality and replacing them with mere pretense, we were shocked but not surprised. Just another footnote[**], this time a jaw-dropper about how in fact the President had been *forced, by Congress,* into his catastrophic war. Despite what we knew, firsthand, from having been there in the audience, having seen the President and his highest subordinates issuing their urgent, saber-rattling warnings and lies, leveraging the gormless worm of Congress into war, triumphally leading us into disaster.

Oops, new version: it never happened.

In my strangled distress I spent more time with Hannah

---

[**] Karl Rove, interviewed on the Charlie Rose television show on November 21, 2007. His revision of history was swiftly rebutted not only by critics but by former White House chief of staff Andrew Card, who appeared on the MSNBC "Morning Joe" television program on November 30 and said "That's not the way it worked."

Arendt (each of us copes differently). She helped me to name these things. Arendt of course produced the monumental analysis of twentieth-century totalitarian regimes and "the relatively recent phenomenon" of "organized lying, dominating the public realm." Most particularly she assessed the Nazi and Soviet practice of "rewriting contemporary history under the eyes of those who witnessed it." Mere factuality is no obstacle for the propaganda regime – indeed, "every known and established fact can be denied or neglected if it is likely to hurt the image."

Surely no further listing of recent abuses of our own propaganda regime is necessary. We do recall, don't we – despite the white snowstorm of disremembering and dehistorying, we do remember how this President rode lies into a second term, used lies to destroy opponents, begin wars, deny science, purchase journalists, subvert government publications. Sometimes he stared into the camera and uttered conscious lies that he himself would publicly reverse just days later*** – weirdly confident that this would make no difference, at least not to his Followers, for whom reality

---

*** President Bush, November 1, 2006: at his press conference, stated that Secretary of Defense Rumsfeld and Vice President Dick Cheney "are doing fantastic jobs and I strongly support them." Bush also "replied in the affirmative when asked if he wanted Rumsfeld and Cheney to stay with him until the end" (Associated Press news reports).

President Bush, November 8, 2006: announced Rumsfeld's resignation. According to *Media Matters* (9 November 2006): "On the November 8 edition of ABC's *World News*, ABC News chief White House correspondent Martha Raddatz noted that "[j]ust one week ago, Mr. Bush said he expected Rumsfeld to remain as secretary to the end of his presidency," adding that "[t]oday, the president acknowledged that he had misled the press."

continued to be . . . whatever the Leader said it was. Just as Arendt described.

What I wish to assert is the non-triviality of this experience: No, we're not crazy, this has indeed been an ideologically driven assault on the foundations of decency.

A propaganda regime uses lying as an organ of state power. It tries to displace and destroy all the little centers of individual power that might dare to exist and thus rival it or challenge its lies. When discourse is undermined and debased – our ability to talk freely together, establish the common ground of our experience, compare notes and validate our sense of things – and replaced with secret surveillance, shouted slogans, topsy-turvy claims, and loyalty tests, then we too begin to fade. For it seems to me that the individual's existence is paradoxically dependent on the healthy togetherness of the read and spoken and heard. When colloquy is denied, our individuality begins to attenuate – we become isolated, wraithlike. What larger self is then left us, except perhaps to become part of the mob, a fan of the State, ready to cheer or march? In this condition we no longer consider what the truth of our existence is. We simply salute. Or shout *Yay*!

Lest this seem like exaggeration, recall: Over half the electorate of 2004 believed a thoroughly discredited untruth about Saddam Hussein's alliance with Al Qaeda (coupled with an equally obvious reversal of which candidate had served his country honorably in uniform). This was in sober fact more of a mob than an electorate. The propaganda assault worked. And it didn't need uniformed goons. Complicit journalists were available to repeat lies for free.

I asked what it means, for leaders to mislead, and for a populace to be willfully blind. We have history to tell us. Here is Arendt:

> The ideal subject of totalitarian rule is not the convinced follower, but people for whom the distinction between fact and fiction (*i.e.* the reality of experience) and the distinction between true and false (*i.e.* the standards of thought) no longer exist.

Too many citizens have given up "common and factual reality itself" (in Arendt's phrase), and replaced it with ideological clichés or a shoulder-shrugging acceptance of absurdity. And the government is trying hard to keep the rest of us mute, fearful (what color terror today?), and off-balance. We have that queasy sensation because "the sense by which we take our bearings in the real world – and the category of truth vs. falsehood is among the mental means to this end – is being destroyed."

> [C]onsistent lying, metaphorically speaking, pulls the ground from under our feet and provides no other ground on which to stand.

Silently we check the eyes of other citizens to see if they've found the secure mark to navigate by. Solid ground seems to have given way. If we're alone, we yell at the TV like we're drowning. We are.

\* \* \*

## 2. Leaving the Party

As I write, I strive to temper my outrage, knowing that ranting won't be readable, won't get me anywhere useful. I admit my frailty: I am a cracked and nearly-broken vessel. It's a marvel I've lasted this long! Or a testament to the blessed powers of healing we are heirs to, we soft humans living on this difficult planet.

I began to understand this about myself, both the cracking and the healing, some decades ago, in another moment of dreadful clarity. I had graduated from an evangelical college and was trying hard to hold together some shreds of my born faith against the plain witness of my life and senses. And among my little group of college friends, tragedy struck: a couple – newlyweds hardly a year together – lost their infant son.

I can only imagine such a loss. A parent's love is something I witness from the outside, with a sense of awe at its risks and burdens. Nonetheless, my epiphany was not about love: It was about pretending. This young couple, scrubbed, middle-class, relentlessly cheerful like much of that Christian gang, reacted most strangely to their loss. They smiled broadly. They held hands and looked placidly forward at us, or into each other's eyes. "We're not grieving" they said. "Because we know he's with Jesus now. And what could be better than that?"

I stared: Nope, not kidding. Not, evidently, trying to keep from crying. Nothing but smiles: nothing but ideology, where human hearts should be. Nothing but Official Belief and Official Language, in place of feeling, however agonized. And to all appearances, this thoroughly-brainwashed pair had no awareness of their own disconnectedness.

What ideology costs us is only *everything*: the right to experience our lives first-hand in all their spontaneity, pain, confusion, joy, and freshness. This loss of humanity is the fortress of true-believing. Within this entrenchment in abstraction, there is no possibility of questioning. When experience is replaced by dogma, whence would a question arise? When language is mere repetition of approved clichés, what words could fashion it? And with no human experience to draw one into compassion, what prevents such a person from doing any kind of violence, any outrage, called for by the pure logic of its system?

Starting with this inner violence done to themselves.

I saw it clearly, with horror. I stood mute, and thirty years later the moment is still vivid to me. Because I could also see how narrowly I had been delivered from this fate. I am one who can say, as if reading the scripture: The truth set me free.

When I was fifteen I had a formal session with myself, a sit-down self-intervention. What is this I'm feeling? I asked. What is its name? A born-again fundamentalist believer, I felt horrified at my own answers, and I wrote the words "I AM A HOMOSEXUAL" on a slip of paper (immediately destroyed) in order to force a reckoning. For the next ten years I sustained my virginity (though certainly not my purity) with strict solitary prayer, Bible reading, and a monk-like self-discipline in eye and act. My commitment was to see and tell myself *the truth* in every life instance. I felt this would be an acceptable sacrifice, a warrant of my spiritual sincerity and a shield against sinning. I attempted to be unsparing, vigilant. Of course I failed and failed. But this attempt itself seems to have been some kind of gift, a moral intensity that sustained truthful thinking – or at least the *intent* of truthful thinking – even while I lied my ass off to everyone around me, terrified of being branded and outcast (a fissuring disjuncture of truth and falseness that made me increasingly strange and angry and depressed, as you could imagine).

But eventually, inevitably, that truth-demanding inner voice began to interrogate my lived experience. If I am wrong and bent, why doesn't Jesus change me? And later (after countless vigils and unanswered prayers), the question – How, exactly, am I worse than other people?

At last, in graduate school, surrounded by friendly non-believing folk, I began to accept that ordinary human life, including gay people and unChristian people, was not the horror of my Baptist imagining. Rather, it was simple and honest and far less viciously convoluted. It was truer. And with that conclusion to my hellish decade of self-reckoning, I turned outward, opened the doors and windows of my awful loneliness and self-loathing, and commenced my real life.

\* \* \*

What connection between this personal odyssey and our slow-motion national emergency of quasi-fascism? Reading Hannah Arendt from this perspective reminds me that totalitarian systems such as Communism or Nazism are, in effect, religions – with orthodox beliefs, heresies, faith, zealotry, and righteousness. It's a common observation, but seldom pursued the next step. What *kind* of religions are they?

Answer: fundamentalist. Classic communism, for instance, demanded blind, total, unthinking loyalty to the cause, and trained its followers to deaden themselves to feeling, experience, evidence, and logic – since these must often contradict the tenets of belief. In Stalinist Russia, or contemporary North Korea: the closed box of fundamentalism, offering all-or-nothing membership at the price of everything.

So, applying the insight in reverse, we can say that fundamentalisms are *totalitarian belief systems*, more alike than different wherever they appear – jihadist Moslems, Bible-pounding Baptists, Hassidic Jews, Bolshevists, Nazis. Any of them will throw out a questioner rather than embrace the possibility of humane dialogue, will exclude or even murder in the name of an invisible Doctrine. Applying Arendt's analysis to the religious right in America is surely more than merely metaphoric. It is an exact description of the phenomenon we find in warmaking and torture-justifying neoconservatives, in "loyal Bushies," and in fervent megachurches all over the land: the totalizing form of belief that snuffs out immediate experience and undermines the power of challenging, truth-seeking thought.

And this analysis gives me some understanding of myself, too. If I acknowledge myself as a refugee, more or less damaged in transit, then I find it easier to comprehend my outbursts of arrogant, careening rage at people who, for reasons I cannot fathom, simply do not possess the hunger for truth, who do not demand it of themselves or of others, who rest comfortably in convenient lies. It is, of course, traumatic reflex. Truth saved me. I cannot release my grip.

To this day, I am far too reactive. *Truth matters!* I want to shout – when nitwits begin comparing their astrological signs at dinner parties. I cannot forgive their cavalier attitude about distinguishing *true* from *not-true.* I am rapt by the beauty of our provisional, mortal kind of knowing, that grey scale in which all our judgments are made – which, though imperfect, rely on canons of shared evidence and rationality that are far, far better than idle guesswork and wishful pretending. Even among my circle of educated professional and artistic friends, all manner of nonsense is trotted out without shame or resistance from others – shamanism and apparitions and crystals and magic healing powers and . . . Good progressives and liberals, they are no fundamentalists but they contribute to the culture of truthlessness too. If I am not to get in red-faced shouting matches, I have to leave the party.

❖ ❖ ❖

### 3. Remember

If I think about myself, my scarred, scared, and too-often unloving inner life; or about that young bereaved couple; or even about our nation reeling in the dust and horror of the Twin Towers; it seems clear that mere epistemology – the technicalities of what truth is and how we know it – is not the end of the discussion. Really it is only the start. At root this is not a problem of information, not a problem of intellect. This is a moral question. A human one.

For you cannot talk about truth without talking about suffering.

What drives a person to adhere blindly to a doctrine, a cult, to become a religious or political fundamentalist and give up so much that is delicious in the human adventure? Surely it is fear, a primal need for safety at all costs. Richard Dawkins (another writer to whom I turn to calm my rage for clarity) concludes that credulous belief is at root a kind of childishness. He offers Isaac Asimov's piercing comment: "Inspect every piece of pseudoscience and you will find a security blanket, a thumb to suck, a skirt to hold." With a philosopher's precision Dawkins refines his search to understand this human failing:

> The quality of childhood that I am trying to pin down is not pure gullibility but a complex combination of gullibility coupled with its opposite – stubborn persistence in a belief, once acquired. The full recipe, then, is extreme early gullibility followed by equally obstinate subsequent unshakeability.

I think we will not soon cure ourselves of delusory beliefs, because this is a hard world, dealing many people more pain and fear than they can bear. The stubbornness, perhaps, we could work on. But the only way I know to do so is with a steady and gentle compassion, easing the grip on this false security. How to do so on a mass scale is beyond me. Though perhaps that is why I have spent so many years writing and teaching – believing (against a great deal of daily evidence) that, reader by reader, student by student, it might help. Maybe that's *my* delusion.

❊ ❊ ❊

I have asked myself, more than once over the last several years – *Is this 1934? And if so, what should I be doing?* But I am unable to answer. In the thick darkness of the present, the crisscross of paths is unreadable. Any one of them might lead to disaster, or a dead end, or perhaps some form of useful resistance. I find it hard to forgive myself or my fellow liberals for being so inept in this charged moment. We fail in the face of falsehoods and manufactured fears while the American experiment in freedom teeters in historic contingency.

Ironically, my great guide Hannah Arendt, so brilliant and so clear in understanding the cataclysms of the immediate past, did no better than us in her own present. She too got lost, could not sort out the human thread from the angry weaving of her time. Confronted with school desegregation in the late 1950s in her adopted American home, she too lost her way. Today we can see the self-evident rightness of the Federal interventions that allowed black children to walk into public schools. Arendt opposed them – for reasons that now look hairsplitting, obtuse, unfeeling.

She got it wrong. We all get it wrong. Only compassion will allow us to stand up from our bewildered stoop, assess our mistakes, beg for forgiveness, bind up the wounds we've suffered and the wounds we've caused. My taxes have gone into the army of empire, have bought the bullets and bombs and sent the soldiers. What fragment of the President's responsibility do I carry? I cannot begin to calculate these moral sums, neither mine nor his. How to tot up the violence this drowning environment of untruth has done to the mind, to the spirit, to all of us? Six hundred thousand dead Iraqis are in some way a quantifiable evil. But a whole nation cut from its moorings? A whole world?

"Justice will take us millions of intricate moves," says William Stafford. And a gesture of forgiveness must begin each one. Recognition of suffering: one's own, one's neighbor's.

What would a politics of compassion look like? Or a personal life, a spirituality, a way of being in the world that was not hard, vigilant, lonely, reactive? This I have hardly begun to know. I have a few notions; I guess we all do, gathered up in glimpses and blessings. I have learned that compassion is concrete, physical, and immediate – undeterred by symbolic battles or abstractions about doctrine. A cup of cold water, some way to be actively present for another's suffering, is surely the golden path open in any moment, any place. If we can but remember to go there.

Some philosophers claim that coming to the truth is but remembering, anyway. If I remember the kindness I have been showered with – how often people have forgiven my hard spirit, my mistakes – will I not *come to* a little quicker? If gratitude replace vigilance, won't the grasp soften, the heart open, the arguing die down?

I'm going there if I can, but I'm going to need a lot of help. We all will.

# *Imagine*

Freshmen are staring at a poem. This is a strange and frightening thing. Through the windows, we are painted briefly in changeable light. Late-winter weather swirls up the Columbia Gorge, reminding Portland of its place in this big world. It's a beautiful moment, somehow poignant. Should be good for poetry.

But I know that some of these students are flatlanding the poem: taking it literally, misunderstanding its metaphors, not hearing its emotion, wondering why it doesn't just say what it means. Others are repelled by the strangeness of someone else's life and mind, the raw inwardness of a lyric poem. "It's ICKY," exclaims one of the resistant ones, rolling her eyes.

In the thirty years since I taught my first undergraduates, I have come to accept this reality of the human spirit: To imagine is difficult. It takes courage – encouragement; it takes opportunities carefully constructed (by me or by the fates). Then something magic happens: A key turns in a lock, eyebrows ascend on foreheads – and a new world is glimpsed, a 3-D moment that dazzles. (That's why one stays in this teaching business.) But there's no guarantee. What you do is lay it before them . . . and wait.

I'm convinced that what teachers are doing, at the level that counts, is not merely delivering knowledge or skills. Secretly, beneath the much-insisted details of biology or poli-sci or poetry, we are awakening the imagination. That big world.

You should see the "Ah!" when a student catches Gerard Manley Hopkins' vision of the god that enkindles even a worn and sullied nature. You should see the tenderness of a suburban kid reliving the epic suffering of a Blackfeet life through a James Welch novel. It's amazing. A kind of grace.

* * *

Imagination is a matter of life and death. It's not just a liberal-arts nicety. If we move forward in our lives (or fail to) it is mostly according to what we can envision. It's true for individuals. It's true for nations, too.

One way to understand our Iraq war, with its terrible costs, is that it happened partly because war-making was the only compelling thing the governing party could imagine doing with the vast wealth and human resources of our nation. If not war, then . . . well, just send the money back. "The American people know best what to do with their own money." Tax cuts. Cuts to health services, to environmental regulation and remediation, to student loans, the poor, even medical research. None of it apparently really worth doing.

The immediate financial cost of this war, through 2007, is about $400 billion. Here's a thought-exercise: What could we have done with that very same money – had we cared to?

Here in Oregon, our share would be about $3.7 billion. With that amount, we could provide health care for 791,185 people (more than a quarter of our small state). Or pay for 64,249 elementary school teachers or 78,277 police officers. Or build 387 elementary schools. Or, if combating terrorism is the point, hire 61,433 port container inspectors. Neighboring Washington would have enough to take out those four salmon-killing Snake River dams, and support redevelopment for ten years. I'm not making this up – I'm cribbing most of it from the National Priorities Project, which has researched these costs and broken them down by state. There's a chart to see what we might have had for our money.

But imagine a candidate having proposed any of these as national priorities in the 2000 presidential campaign. Snorts of derision and disbelief – We can't afford that!

Of course we can't. Unless we decide we can. And then, miraculously, a way is found. It is a matter of choosing.

❊ ❊ ❊

Progressives will always have a harder time making their case because their vision predicates an imaginative leap: that we are, after all, fundamentally *connected* to each other – that my fate and happiness are not private matters only, but a shared project. A tax cut takes no imagination to see: it's a few more bucks in your pocket. But seeing one's ownership in a community, seeing one's own face in someone else's child, that takes imagination. It's an uphill battle in a culture that celebrates a mythic and bellicose individualism.

But we do have some cultural resources to draw on. Go

to a church and try reading aloud: "Who is my neighbor?" Jesus spent a lot of time contradicting that instinctive individualism. Maybe some of us could be persuaded to listen.

Imagine – combining our resources to relieve suffering and to open up dead-ends of poverty and hopelessness. Imagine knowing that our fate is each other.

Imagine – knowing that our fate also swims with the salmon and grows with the trees.

Imagine living beyond yourself, even beyond your bank account. Imagine doing what you're good at and in love with, even if it doesn't pay so well. That would be like coming back to life, wouldn't it? It would be like grace.

Imagine.

# Unlocking the Hips

*Mike*

The track coach told me to "watch Mike's hips," so I ran workouts right behind him. They rocked, they unlocked, those hips gave him a fluid stride and a springy strength. (And lord, that sexy, flexy lower back!)

Coach saw me as underperforming most of the time. It was a high school, he wanted victories, but I was trying the half-mile that year instead of my natural longer events. It was my rebellion. I wanted to be fast and powerful. The long-distance claque plods past, too skinny for words, that open-jawed hangdog look. Mike and I are about to do repeat quarters at sixty seconds. Twelve of them. He's a year older, cool and confident. Coach whistles us on and clicks his stopwatch. Mike has a beautiful stride, efficient, self-contained, powerful. His arms ride low. Hands not clenched. At each stride, the unlocked hip rotates forward and lengthens his reach. He's running from his lower abdomen, each rotation is an uncoiling of the torso's core strength. Guys who run on legs only are left behind.

I'm a very good student and I start running better almost immediately. Mike is much shorter than me, wide-shouldered, lean. His last name is Mexican. The seniors rib each other, bantering and rowdy – laughing, they call him "Nigger" in the shower-room because his penis is almost black with pigment. The rest of him is a beautiful light mahagony. It doesn't matter anyway since Mike wins all his races and is unflappable, suave. They can't touch him.

We only get a minute or two between quarter-miles. I'm deep-trained for distance and hard to tire. I stick without a word, watching Mike's hips.

* * *

*Bob*

"Oates, I *missed* you." His face was exasperated, and the word *missed* landed with flawless deadpan. Underneath was sincere. We had been working together for three weeks without a break, repairing the abandoned camp, sleeping in the crumby bunkhouse, eating the makeshift food. Then a week off. And on coming back for more – this surprising greeting. Who knew a straight boy had feelings?

I was touched but it threw off all my calculations.

Bob was not suave. Homely and skinny, he used to be a nationally ranked marathoner but neither of us was competing any more. Now we were mountaineers. Sort of.

Once he came and sat on the edge of my cot, an hour or two after lights out, asking if I was okay. He didn't exactly know I had finally cracked that night – tears on the pillow, frustration I almost couldn't bear. None of my calculations made me strong enough. Bob saw something, something. I kept meeting men who extended kindness to me, like they were unafraid. I didn't expect it, didn't know it was out there. How then should I be?

It was exasperating. The next day as we hiked along, dusty and silent, I just started laughing. I never told him why.

* * *

*Carny*

Santa Barbara was a hot long hitchhike from San Francisco once our Spring Break getaway was over. When the battered Nova stopped I jumped in the passenger side while Harry and the backpacks took the rear. The driver – I remember thinking *He's got a nice head of hair for such an old guy.*

He said he was a carny. "You know what that is? Carny?" He shouted at us, all the windows down in the heat and doing a very noisy, bouncing-and-gliding seventy. This was on 101, with all its patches and old paving. He gave me a huge blunt handshake and I realized he wasn't old but just *worked*, hard-worked and weathered. He figured us instantly, no doubt, for what we were.

He was a carnival foreman, had done it for a long time. "I've seen everything. Everything. You know?" I didn't but guessed that I did. I never felt less menace from anyone in my life. He was almost fatherly. Motherly. Of course I was on guard, being who I was, but I followed the carny's thread, as we drove, like it was a thin cool stream. He talked on, the kind of men who work a carnival then drift off, the way he woke up one day and felt he had seen enough unkindness for three lifetimes.

Then he brought up Nixon. He leaned over, still not menacing but I hated to think where this would end up. We were long-haired and scared of what we called rednecks. "Stay out of that damn war. Stay in school, that's good." He asked if I knew how many Vietnamese we had killed, how many GIs. "We're going to kill a lot more before that s.o.b. is done." He was not arguing, just shouting over the freeway.

"That Mao – in China? I know we're supposed to hate him. But you know what I think? I think he fed his people." He looked at me to see if I registered. "It's a poor country. He fed his people."

There were no stickers on his back bumper, nothing to give him away. It was late cool dusk, we were outside Atascadero and we knew a girl to call there. The carny blinked on his lights and waved backwards at us as he pulled out.

❖ ❖ ❖

*The T'ai Chi Instructor*
The t'ai chi instructor does not hurry. He is not lunging, and not not lunging either.

The t'ai chi instructor is not seen as the observer wills.

The t'ai chi instructor is on the balls of his feet, shifting weight. When he pushes the air, I believe it. When he rotates, everything rotates.

The t'ai chi instructor's tummy peeks out, fuzzy, fleshy. He is not a Greek god. His t-shirt comes a little short, it's what he wore to teach a roomful strangers.

His body is not a vehicle, not an advertisement, it doesn't project anything – power, or glamour, or masculinity. Or even sexiness – which of course could be quite sexy. He might be thirty, and I'm almost double that. It's my first t'ai chi ever.

It could be dancing, really. His spine is loose and his hips fluid. Not like those professional dancers on TV – those gimbaled manlings, those palomino women. I don't know what that is. This is nice. Amazing.

The t'ai chi instructor is the kind of guy you can't tell what kind of guy he is. He smoothes through one move and connects it to the next. I'm so bad at this it should bother me. But think how good I must make the others feel! I've had good teachers, and he's another. He bends, uncoils, there's that lower-abdomen place again. All the power is in there, behind the fuzz. For a while, I ran from that place.

I'm the stiffest person in the room, but I feel a willow. Bull-willow. Sissy-willow. I might get better at this, who knows?

# Banner Peak

Just a quick step-around, face-in to the rock. Day pack well snugged, no chance of balance-shift. Three sliding sidesteps. A spray of gravel and sand, two stones that ping . . . ping . . . splonk into the banked snow around a blue-green tarn, way far down. I glance down briefly, unwisely, past my left boot.

Not supposed to have to do this on Banner Peak.

Then the last step is taken and I sit for a few moments. Wedge of blue, quiet sky above rusty broke-rock jumble-scape. Sawtoothed ridges, like those famous Minarets not quite visible from here. Slip off the pack, swallow some water. On a narrow bench of basalt, fanny-damp and cold even at mid-summer, I'm joined by a surprising crowd of gentian, penstemon, polemonium, trying their variations of deep-blue-purple. *Did you know I'd be coming up today?* I ask them. You can behave foolishly when you're alone and the world is big around you. I consider the strange rock, full of ringing iron, dark as tophet, prone to splintering. Upwards I see steep talus and a long snowfield. I brought my ice-axe for that. Nothing technical, just a little safety margin.

More water and a handful of gorp. A luxuriance descends upon me.

\* \* \*

Banner Peak is really just a walk-up, not even thirteen thousand feet. What a laugh. So I laugh – why not? I want a leg-stretcher, a chance to breathe and look. All my hard mountains are behind me, I'm beginning to suspect. This little one seems a big enough pleasure for now.

The summit is windy and bright, the world wide. Down there I can see my starting point, the lake where my old friend Madeleine has agreed to spend her *wilderness solo day*, as she mock-heroically insists. She's not a mountain gal, not one bit, she's Fairfax High, Santa Monica, a foodie and a softish almost-fifty. Yet she backpacked a long altitude-gaining day with me to arrive at that classic mountain setting, where we set up camp, she almost giddy with fatigue but game as always, out of her comfort zone *By choice*, she said – wanting to experience the Sierras before she got any older.

It's a grand lake for the altitude, from here a broad blue dotted with rock-islands, edged with stands of lodgepole and open stony lookouts. I hope she's enjoying it. She owned a certain irrational fear of being alone down there. Fair enough, I said. *Don't wander far* was my only advice.

In the other direction, just a half-mile down the ridgeline, stands craggy Mt. Ritter. Quite astonishing from this vantage. Briefly I wonder why I am not over there following John Muir's footsteps . . . *Like a real man*. But that's an old mumble I've stopped believing. On the grim-black and difficult peak, Muir recorded his remarkable first ascent, a famous story right up there with his climbing-a-tree-in-a-windstorm and his inching-across-the-glacier. A few years earlier Clarence King had been turned back by Ritter's last five hundred feet. Unclimbable! he'd said. Muir never hesitated of course, though he came at last to these heroics:

> I was suddenly brought to a dead stop, with arms outspread, clinging close to the face of the rock, unable to move hand or foot either up or down. My doom appeared fixed. I *must* fall. There would be a moment of bewilderment, and then a lifeless tumble down the one general precipice to the glacier below.

It's a good story, even in Muir's Victorian style. Because in the next moment he enters that strange zone of hyper-attention and calm in which great athletes and people in mortal distress perform miracles. "Every rift and flaw in the rock was seen as through a microscope, and my limbs moved with a positiveness and precision with which I seemed to have nothing at all to do . . ."

What follows is amazing – deliverance, summit, beatitude of light. It is a dangerous world threaded with salvation that Muir describes.

On my forgotten summit, when I get there, a powerbar for lunch. More gorp (raisins and peanuts, home-mixed). Lots of water. Far below at that glinting lake is my friend, her life story spooled out invisibly behind her, down the trail and into the past. She raised two boys alone when the dad went absent, and got a Ph.D. from UCLA as she did so. This was just before liberation changed things. When she went to the bank, the manager wouldn't open an account *unless your husband or your father will sign.* She reports dismissiveness, sideways looks, plodding forward. Exhaustion, loneliness, determination.

The boys turned out magnificently.

Heroic is a relative term, I decide.

Later, coming down to the steparound bottleneck once more, I find I can toss my knapsack over – carefully – and maneuver unencumbered but sure, like a bigfooted ballerina. I feel a rare joy at glimpsing again the big islandy lake where Madeleine is waiting, surprising myself at the anticipation of comradeship, the sharing of stories. *I saw a bird,* she'll say. I saw a flower, a view. We'll make miso soup and then my knockout trail dinner, tortellini and abundant parmesan and oregano, with fresh basil smuggled in. No mountain was ever less important than this one under my boots, barely a bump on my list of deeds, yet when did I ever feel so happy, about to share life with a warmhearted friend?

# Un-Hating the Muir Trail

For the first time I can see it as something beside an open wound.

How many years, though, did I struggle against it, hating it, avoiding it. Starting four decades ago in my teens, it seemed that half the art of planning a hiking trip was figuring a route that would spend minimum time, or none at all, on the suddenly too-famous, too-traveled trail. My climbing and hiking pals all agreed: Stay off it. We went to extraordinary lengths of ingenuity, crossing ridges off-trail, linking up good places in unheard-of ways, all to avoid the crowded contamination of the John Muir Trail.

Up and down 211 miles of the southern Sierra, the famous John Muir Trail had become a scar tearing open a high green meadow, an engineer's zigzag razored into a hillside, an ache of remorse, an infuriation of tourists, a loss of pristine beauty. In some places, it could be worn down two feet lower than the surround, and then another set of tracks would develop along both sides to avoid spring mud, which themselves turned into rutbogs in time, and then another pair would appear further out yet, a five-lane sign of human passing, agh, horse-hoof, mule-dropping, Vibram print, tennis tread, dung fresh, dung dried, dung ground into ground, then by August ankle-deep dust in place of linear bog choking the middle track, the trudging footworn airborne leaf-silting poreclogging smudge of people, people, people.

Then you'd raise your eyes and see the hills, the mountains. The granite cliffs and ridgelines you'd actually come to be with. *There*, you'd think. *No one up there.* Some days you might just take a 90-degree turn off the trail and cross-country up, over, away. Topo map might say there was a brook to find, a tiny valley notched under a peak, and off you'd go.

At that point you would notice, right away, how just two or three strides off the Muir Trail it was, well, pretty much pristine. Meadow grass going to yellow, sprinkles of cinquefoil, meadowfoam, aster. Lodgepoley forest grazing the meadow's edge, then maybe Jeffrey Pine bigger, quieter, mixed with who knows what because by now you're climbing, looking for that brook, and then when you find it you're working up the drainage, you can see the peaks above, a few hours pass, some scrambling, and then you're there. Panting, sweaty under the backpack, finishing off your water. Looking around. What's here? Just another meadow, greener and smaller than the one below. Maybe you're in a wide flat where a glacier once worked its icy bottom into the bedrock, settling from the cirque all around while preparing to grind off down-valley. So tarns in the granite, stream splashing through, limber pine, stands of mountain hemlock, gentian. Perfect, really.

And where, exactly, to pitch the bright nylon tent? Even though you're tired, you'll do a search. Rest the pack somewheres, sit a minute, sure, but then a nice slow stiff-legged wander, checking out the neighborhood and above all seeking that archetype or template, *the good place*: big trees or cliff in back, a little clearing, elevation over mildly sloping ground, a stream or a lake's edge in front. Views will provide breadth of thought and a sense of safety. That's what you want. It is a coign, a corner, a nook where you can see but not be seen. It's written into your mind somewhere near the brainstem, older than language I think. So you don't fight it too much, taking time to look until the mental bell goes off: *Ah, here.*

Now the strange part: "Ah here" will suddenly, unexpectedly, show signs of previous visitors. People. Yes it will. How many times did I have to admit this, despite my hour's or my day's off-trail exertions? More than I can count. I came to understand (grudgingly) that our minds were all mapping this place the same way. I saw that human habitat preferences were distinct, strongly marked. No matter how far off-trail, I found that I drifted effortlessly toward nooks containing the signs of other people, sometimes other people altogether since I saw the obsidian flakes and arrowheads they left – but the same mind. Our mind.

Truth be told, despite my stated purpose in those days to avoid all tourists and find the untrodden way, these places, with their slight charcoal hints and fire-rings, were always good spots, excellent spots. And that nagging *need* I always felt that nattered and whispered all the more insistently if I was tired and it had been a long explore to get there, *findagoodplace, getagoodplace, getasafeplace* . . . as long as no one else was physically present, it actually contented me

– though I would never admit it – to settle in a place with this slight warming touch of the human about it. No, certainly would never admit it. But there it was.

* * *

Maybe that was the beginning of my change of heart about the Muir Trail, too.

Think of what produces a trail: human feet. Augmented by pack animals, yes. But mostly human feet, a steady stream of feet, leather boots, Gore-tex boots, lightweight or heavyweight, imprinting a big load or a little load, fast toe-gouging pace or plodwise heel-thudding pace, a perpetual bipedal cascade coursing up and down the trailway. Regular streams – of water – are produced by gravity: first sun, then wind and a few other elementary dynamics, then gravity. Down it comes, down blindly seeking down, and (miraculously) producing snowbanks, tarns with tadpoles, silverdollar cirque-lakes, waterfalls, cascades, meanders, trout pools, and all the rest of it. Amazing – just water gravitating, trying to go down. Whatever "gravity" turns out to be (and the explanations so far are pretty abstruse, Einsteinian space-bending, gravity waves, and so on), it works out rather well, doesn't it?

A trail is created by equally invisible and hard-to-define forces. A stream of human footfalls is driven by a force of will and intention. Its gravity is desire. It can go up as well as down. Its elementary dynamics include longing, hearsay, loneliness, sociableness, love, curiosity, the lust of the eye and the pride of life.

Crossing the Great Western Divide, the Muir Trail ends

on Mt. Whitney, the high point of the continent south of Alaska. Think of it: a stream of desire flowing upwards right to the summit.

And why not see this, too, as beautiful? A river of human beauty splashing and coursing through some of the most *un*human beauty imaginable. Or not unhuman, exactly, but maybe more-than-human, trans-human beauty. Our little current of loving hiking seeing just one thread in the hugest of evermoving tapestries, peaks and valleys, carpenter ants and fir needles, gravities and carbon cycles . . . and us.

\* \* \*

From his perch above Yosemite Valley John Muir once wrote a prayer for humans he pitied, down in their populated places:

> Pat, pat, shuffle, shuffle, crunch, crunch, I hear you all on the sidewalks and sandbeds, plodding away, hoping in righteousness and heaven, and saying your prayers as best you can . . . Heaven help you all and give you ice and granite.

Well, those very people, down there in San Francisco, soon answered his prayer: They read Muir's articles – founded the Sierra Club – followed him to the Sierras – and Lo, the John Muir Trail appeared. A stream of geo-athletico-spiritual aspiration flowed upwards from the towns and hot lands below, crossed meadows, zigzagged up mountains, found passes where the aspirants paused, wind cutting tears to their eyes, eyes recording blessings to their minds, and whose blessings if not Muir's? – who had spoken better than he knew. Like me, he would have hated the Trail, would have disdained all those people. Those tourists. (He mocked them and their late-Victorian fashions and dalliances, fiercely, as they poured into Yosemite and its approaches.)

Yes. I learned it from him, that youthful disdain for the John Muir Trail. That unreasoning rejection of my kind, my kin, in the mountains.

But now I've come to un-learn it. People have been in these mountains for centuries, for millennia: Miwok crossing to trade with Paiute and Yana recrossing to meet, perhaps, Tubatulabel, and who knows who before them. So add bare feet to the pathmaking. You could look it up: Anthropologists are finding signs of habitation easily three thousand years old all along the western foothills. And that's surely the merest hint of what went on here. The paths now trudged by backpackers, loaded with aluminum gimmicks and nylon shelters, are often the very footways which leatherclad hunters and traders and heat-avoiding lowlanders have followed since the end of the last ice age brought them south into this agreeable land with its welcoming summer mountains. We belong here.

Muir taught us to imagine empty forests as Edens in which we could be Adams. He hated seeing Indians in his mountains in the 1860s and 70s. They always made him morose and unkind. They spoiled his illusion.

I'm ready to know better now. I will see no wound, no unwelcome intrusion. I'm in my fifties and I'm looking forward to picking up where I left off decades ago, when I fled the Sierras (too crowded) for the Cascades (empty, or at least emptier). I have in mind a stretch of Muir Trail I always stayed away from, though it runs through some of the best mountain country on the continent: Evolution Valley. I've been near it a few times, on cunningly-designed routes of solitary off-trail avoidance. But this time, walking a lot slower to be sure, I'll try thinking of the populous trail as just one of the ways mountains are used by living creatures, a thin thread of seasonal visitation dotted with brightly-colored, occasionally obnoxious, blissed-out, thinking-of-dinner two-legged visitors, who will be surrounded, each and every one, by deft crowds of whirring mosquitoes, raucous Clark's jays, darting chipmunks and ground squirrels all eager to utilize these large, predictable mammals holding their guide books open, staring at plants and peaks and stars, mouths gaping in awe . . . as their candy bars and trailmixes are pillaged and carried back to ground-nests or tree-nests. And most of the time they won't even mind.

Some evening this next summer, in the gloaming time of camp-making and dinner-cooking, I will stand to straighten my back for a moment and notice before me that stream of trodden earth shining across the meadow and into the tree-line, following a course laid with unerring leg-wit, avoiding unnecessary exertion, finding the best route, as certain as water, as inevitable as desire. I'll see it differently this time.

# Things I Have Experienced but Do Not Believe In

About such things I may be trusted in an oddly backward way because I know too little to fake them. Few people ever had less truck with New-Agery or any other credulous nonsense, religious or otherwise. I don't know how to get Jupiter aligned with Mars. I cannot track my past lives. I don't know The Secret. I don't know which crystal does what – or which aroma, which food-allergy, which bad thought, good thought, mantra, demon, angel, engram, chant, or anything. All as opaque to me as several coats of interior latex.

And yet. There are those happenings that strike us as wondrous and inexplicable. That cause us to reach, *reach* for some magnitude of explanation that feels as potent and spacious as the experience itself. Some of what I've experienced seems to be the stuff of which very exotic explanatory systems are fashioned. But I record only. My eyebrows are up to here, I'm amazed myself. And I have not the faintest idea what it all means.

There's that chi-ball in your lower abdomen. When I began noticing it, I had never even heard the word "chi," and later I kept confusing it with ceramic pets that grew green pelts. But years of running had put me into some mighty inward body-connected awarenesses. I felt, physically, that right *there* was where it was happening. What? Oh, on a good run, a point of tensile balance, a deep power source. Often by the end of an arduous workout it had drifted off, fragmented, my limbs and torso weren't orchestrating themselves any more and I was back to being a tired collection of parts. But there had been *something* . . .

Or - Once I was walking up a meadowed alpine valley and felt the sameness of my flesh with that of the grasses and trees et cetera. A painfully hackneyed point . . . yet some shift had occurred in my sense of body-mind-world and – rather than just mentally *knowing* this truism – I breathed and felt the absolute literalness of it. When the Brahms Requiem quotes the New Testament – *all flesh is grass* – I register only the metaphor. But in that moment I knew it down there in my gut (again that strange center . . .). Us, birds, bugs, green world. Us.

Words are thin, they too quickly become cant. I believe in the grass, not the moral of the grass. I believe in the power, not the chi.

* * *

If you live long enough you will be battered with nearly unendurable pain. My tribulations have been relatively light, but they've almost crushed me at times. It's a wonder any of us makes it.

I had a painful "divorce" (we weren't allowed to marry) after nine years. It just devastated me. Who knows why but at forty years old I was alone, alone. Lost my job, too. My buddy Peter the Chinese Medicine guy saw me spiraling down, and asked if he could "practice" his massage techniques on me. This was friendly pretending – he was offering free therapy. And I took it.

There was something going on with his hands – So help me, I could feel it. Later I learned that the palms of the hands (in eastern medical thinking) are a "chakra" whence "energy" might emanate. These words have no measurable or definable meaning, I insist. Yet a palpable heat came out of them, and week by week I felt Peter imparting a kind of *momentum* to me, as if the body might be working to heal the spirit. (Or "spirit," since I don't know what that is either.)

In time I moved away, determined to start over in a new town. After a year of separation, my unresolved love for my former partner still felt overpowering. In limbic moments – while waking, or doing nothing in particular – I kept seeing it as a silver cord that came out of my sternum and arced over the thousand intervening miles straight into his heart. It was real, it was physical, it seemed as solid as any perception I'd ever had. Whatever this cosmic extension-cord was, it affirmed something vitally important to me.

Of course, they call the heart a chakra too. Wouldn't you know.

* * *

Or this. I was making my way alone across a neat little plateau in the Sierras – one of those places you can notice on a map and dream about, a little land in the sky cut off by steeps and ridges. No trail. Late in the afternoon I had reached the far edge: My plan was to descend to the turquoise-rimmed lake below, named Sphinx because of the towered-up cliffs and formations that backed it. There I stood, staring down. Experience told me *there's always a way* and so there I was, nosing along, trying this chute, that buttress. Stopping. Backtracking. As long as you're patient it's fine, pushing back the little stabs of anxiety, keeping focus, not getting over-committed to a bad route.

In horizontal light I emerged at last exhausted, exhilarated, onto the sage-dotted slopes below the cliffs. Those are big spaces, and it felt weirdly significant simply to stand there, delivered from the vulnerability of the body one more time, breathing in the odor of white sage crushed under my boots, watching a hawk wheeling far out over the lake. Then, when the moment had fully expanded, I saw a solitary buck across the sweep of downslope, at just my elevation, slowly turning his big-racked head, picking his way through the green and sere rockscape in golden light.

I can't really say what it meant. But the sage smelled like blessing – resiny, fragrant, unexpected. I can smell it still.

This was before my little round of heartbreak. I had no idea – no one ever does – how much blessing I would soon be needing. Nor how much I would find, stronger than my obtuseness and deeper than any jargon or borrowed mysticism: blessing woven it seems right into us, and into all the world besides.

# Red Door

FEBRUARY 2008

Within the ancient walls of Sarlat, a modest French town amidst the mountain-edged river-country of the Dordogne, stands a medieval building. Pointed arches, weathered Gothic stonework, I saw it in my wanderings and thought it must be a church. It was once – but it's had a brutal history, including a stint as an arms and gunpowder manufactory in Revolutionary days. Today it's a public market, an airy roofed hall with a wideopen double entrance-way.

But something remarkable has been added to the portal: three-story doors in two vast pointed leaves of grey steel. Standing open for *marché* mornings, or rumbled shut, they're modernist gestures that somehow define the Gothic space as nothing else ever has. They are severe, truthful, and utterly unexpected: our present moment speaking to our past. And across them in blood-red letters, this line from Baudrillard: "L'architecture est un mélange de nostalgie et d'anticipation extrême."

In France I may almost escape the torture regime whose passport I carry. A medieval town – yes here is the nostalgia. But anticipation *extrême*? The words lodge in me, the doors loom in my memory, a fusion of intellect and beauty and ordinary moneymaking. Melange indeed.

\* \* \*

One day a half-year later, back in the States, it becomes
finally and unmistakably clear that no one will ever be held
to account for our government's crimes. A vote is taken, a
craven opposition folds. And something breaks in me – some
long-held naïveté about my country, its decency and prom-
ise. It is an ordinary day, just another political skirmish, but
I am suddenly hollowed out, perilously close to depression.
A three-day funk, let's call it, when the ugly brutality beneath our fine prosperous surfaces seems stripped bare and
exposed.

I think I must have been seduced, these many years –
blinded from seeing deeper – by those most beautiful words
of Jefferson and Madison. The language and apparatus of
democracy, so beautiful, so ringing. Are they not our Sistine,
our "David," our ecclesiastical Gothic, convincing even from
centuries away? The Declaration's Preamble, *We hold these
truths, created equal.* And the system – on paper – of bal-
anced and self-checking governance. And the two-hundred-
year process – again, on paper – of bringing democracy forward, Fourteenth Amendment, Nineteenth Amendment . . .
I see now, far too clearly: Jefferson and Madison are our
poor traduced Michelangelos and Leonardos, hired to deco-
rate a thug state. Their founding fantasias are not in marble
and paint but in the words and aspirations that form this
vacant temple of democracy.

Within the temple the same bloody hand rules. Sforza,
Medici, Robespierre, Jackson, Nixon, Bush. Washington

and Clinton. All of them. Even the good ones were only pretending to steer, while wealth flowed upwards protected by force of arms. No president – not Obama, not anyone – will challenge this system.

And I am a five-decade fool, dazzled by a pretty cloud of words. We love the *Duomo* and the "David" of Renaissance Florence, can't help it, irresistible. We forget their owners, those dark-eyed Sforzas and Medicis peering down from their tower just behind, clad in black leather, steel swords edged and ready. Laughing at the artists, the writers, the gullible humanists with their hopes.

❖ ❖ ❖

I write these words on the Hawthorne Bridge, walking in a long midsummer evening toward a theatrical event. Perhaps it will relieve me of thinking, I'm thinking. But when I turn the corner and see the rough-hewn rock and *faux* battlements of the Portland Armory – one of our best buildings, marvelously renovated, green, civic . . .

. . . the stab sinks all the way home. This is of course our 1891 relic, originally built to reassure the merchant class that the National Guard would protect them. From whom? From the citizenry of course. Arms, rifles, cannons: It was the era of the Homestead Strike, the Pullman Strike. *Hundreds of thousands* of impoverished workers in the streets over the preceding decade. The Haymarket massacre. The might of Federal and State Governments brought to crush – to bayonet and shoot and jail and judicially strangle – this workers' movement. For whom? For those who already had wealth, those who had, after all, just brought machine-pol

President Benjamin Harrison to office despite his losing the popular vote. Harrison visited Portland that very year and reviewed the Guard approvingly, the bearded embodiment of systematic corruption. Before his presidency he had not merely been a railroad lawyer prosecuting unions. He had organized and commanded a force of soldiery against them.

It is a strange thing to see the edgy-beautiful interior of the Armory now, turned into a theatrical space, hung with odd and richly colored modernist paintings. Strange to take in the Shakespeare, the Isherwood, the sharp-tongued stagings of contemporaries. A pleasure of intellect and spirit. Afterwards I find dinner with friends, then walk myself back over the bridge in the dark, moved by the commitments of so many – playwright, actors, hell even fundraisers. Their passions, their years in pursuit, unrelenting. Something beautiful arises from this place of oppression.

Resurrection isn't automatic. It is real, but it takes an act of extreme imagination, steely and wholly unlikely.

\* \* \*

Sarlat, the town with the big-doored market-church, was the home of one of the most lamented friends in literary history, Etienne de la Boëtie. I saw his name memorialized on another building by the square and had to sit down. *This is where it happened*? I asked myself. It was none other than Michel de Montaigne who experienced the loss of this friend – a nearly mortal blow. At the age of thirty-eight, distraught, Montaigne gave up politics (he had been mayor of Bordeaux) and retired to country life. By his account, theirs had been a noble friendship, a rare meeting of minds and hearts. Bereft,

Montaigne faced emptiness, despair.

From this deep darkness, he started writing. I have the book here: the *Essays.* In his grief, in retreat from the slaughterhouse years of the 1570s and 80s – the decay of Renaissance into blood-red massacre – Montaigne literally invented the personal essay. He called it "the only book of its kind . . . wild and fantastically eccentric." Personally revealing, honest to the heart, wandering wherever the mind went: a true picture of a living intellect. Nothing like such essays had ever been seen. But people have been writing them ever since.

The new door must be discovered, invented, magicked into being. *Then* you walk through it. Without creative transformation, an end is just . . . the end.

Somewhere in France a man's friend dies. A great heart is broken, and he takes up the pen. Three hundred years later, on the edge of a faraway continent, someone else writes from his own confusion and longing, trying to find his way. He stands on a bridge in the darkness, or on the edge of a mountain. And here it is, in your hand: the personal essay, as Montaigne invented it. A mere leaf, a little door, the endpage of a thousand magazines, the last word, the invitation, *l'envoi.*

History moves sideways. Resurrection isn't automatic. It takes an act of extreme imagination, steely and wholly unlikely.

We live in a time of national and international thuggery, much of it in our name, America's name. We have slaughtered and won and lost. We have seen much that we thought solid washed away in floods of state propaganda and militarist bloodymindedness. How many articles of the Bill of Rights? How much torture, how many dead? Who knew America could die so easily?

This is the moment. Where is the door?

# II. RENDERING

# Rendition

JANUARY-MAY 2007

I think I see bodies dropping from the sky. They are tiny fig-
ures, jet-black, perhaps their limbs are flailing, perhaps not,
as they appear in the blue and plummet soundlessly down
and down to vanish into the vastness and bustle of Paris. Yet
it is April and the sky is fair and I am up on the Montmartre,
the Basilica of Sacré-Cœur at my back and all the city at my
feet. Like many others I have prospered during the current
regime and here I am in France for my long stay. I should be
having brighter visions.

Cities seem to be physical entities but they are not. I experience Paris as a translucent dome of language: that rich
medium where vowels and consonants mingle like sung
notes: *temps, timbre, tentacion*. I find it a frustrating and gor-
geous music, after only a few months here, but the French
love their language volubly and all day long bells of sheer
expressive joy are going off around me in the stations of the
Metro, at stands and along sidewalks – *parole* and *langue*,
the rapt incomparability of Paris, *Pah-REE. Comment dit-
on, Paris?*

A different language is a different world. Who are we?

What are we? The roads and roofs here are the same as any-where else. But the answers are not.

As I am writing this it is still the same Spring, in the same France as always, and it is hard to believe how recently the word "rendition" meant only some singer's version of a fa-vorite song, an old story we love to retell.

The falling bodies do not leave visible tears or rents in the fabric of the dome of light and language, the city goes on and I do too. But we know something is changing. A civilization seems to be a physical entity but it is not. It is a set of ideas held in words.

And like all things human, they can only hold up for so long against determined abuse.

*  *  *

**European Parliament - News - Press service
14 February 2007:**
Over one thousand CIA-operated flights used
European airspace from 2001 to 2005 and temporary
secret detention facilities 'may have been located
at US military bases' in Europe, says the European
Parliament in its final report on illegal CIA activities
in Europe, adopted 14 February. The report, which
deplores the passivity of some Member States in the
face of illegal CIA operations, as well as the lack of
co-operation from the EU Council of Ministers, was
approved by a majority of 382 against 256 with 74
abstentions.

The Parliament rejects extraordinary renditions
"as an illegal instrument used by the USA in the fight

against terrorism" and condemns the "acceptance and concealing of the practice, on several occasions, by the secret services and governmental authorities of certain European countries."

\* \* \*

Whenever I come to Paris I go up to see the view from Montmartre and then turn to enter the famous domes of Sacré-Cœur, where Jesus' heart pops out of his body, golden. Off to his right Mary's does the same. They lean over us from the central dome, gaunt and gigantic in *faux*-Byzantine mosaic. To the side, under its own domelet, a wafer of flesh is displayed for adoration. Around back of the altar, other body parts are being rendered – skin flayed, limbs pierced, ribs busted, lungs poked open by a spear, and so forth. It's a festival of cruelty, Station by Station. This ought to be disturbing but it's done rather nicely and I guess we have all seen it before.

I took a seat. It is nice to sit in large human spaces with strangers. And to my surprise I fell to wondering whether I might be a Christian myself.

I had left faith behind decades ago – about the time of my very first visit to Sacré-Cœur, in fact. Yet I recalled that our doctrine (Baptist) was firm: "Once saved always saved." The Blood of Christ was ineradicable. Once you got it on you, it was for good. So I found myself staring up into the architectural religiosity and pondering, perhaps idly: Can one be an unwilling, or unwitting, Christian? For I have no doubt of the realness of my once-upon-a-time salvation. At age thirteen, twenty, even twenty-two I was as *saved* as a human could appear to be. I prayed fervently, daily. I committed many verses to heart and in fact could speed-recite them, in a joshing-competitive sort of way: John 3:16. ForGodSoLovedTheWorldThatHeGaveHisOnlyBegotten . . .

I had even gone door to door with pamphlets and nothing more than a true-believer's gall and an adolescent's determination to do the right thing. In six or seven sentences you were supposed to dispense with another person's entire life experience and deliver unto their hands the salvific words, depicted right there in the literature in cartoon form.

Then move on to the next house.

I could only bear it for one afternoon. I was in ninth grade. Even then I had a good nose for lying and pretending. By the time I was twenty-four I had been rendered out of the church myself, unable to sustain the pretence that prayer was making me heterosexual, unable to believe the lie that God hated me the way the straight fierce believers said.

Below the dome of Jesus' selectively adored internal organs I remembered this. It made me sad and even a little teary, but this was probably just empty sentiment, a product of the place.

\* \* \*

At none of the Stations of the Cross (except the last) was Jesus tortured, according to America's legal reinterpretation of the term. If scourging, beating, and the like do not lead to "major organ failure or death," they are to be considered *enhanced interrogation,* not torture. Used with *extraordinary rendition*, these are instruments of a neoconservative plan for a hundred years of American empire – a sort of

Hundred-Year Reich.

It was a heady vision. Vice President Cheney foresaw Republican dominance and virtual one-party rule for years or even decades. The "Project for the New American Century" (called PNAC by insiders) put it all in writing in 1997, posted it on a website, placed its people in the Bush government – Wolfowitz, Bolton, Rumsfeld, Cheney, and many others – and sprang into action once the proper excuse was provided. PNAC planned for the entire Earth, for a full century to come, to be lorded over by an unchallenged American military projecting an economic empire of unthinkable wealth for the corporate and the well-connected. I'm not making this up – they didn't even bother to hide their plans. War, propaganda, torture, and the other post-constitutional devices of the Unitary Executive are all means to this end: a century of unchallengeable power.

How long does a Hundred-Year Reich last? In the year 2000, PNAC produced a nifty ninety-page manual for world domination. But it's probably fairest to start measuring its brief, bloody life from its first substantial achievement, the invasion of Iraq in March of 2003. The next presidential election (2008) will surely close the books on PNAC's century, just ninety-five years short of the goal.

As with all such overreaching, the end will be sudden – with what human-rights and mass-murder prosecutions it remains to be seen.

Then we will wonder: What was that? Why did we permit this?

✳ ✳ ✳

garantiedesdroitsn'estpasassureenilaseparation

The overarch of language under which we live is made literal in the Metro station Place de la Concorde. Letter by letter, tile by tile, in an all-over design from platform to platform right across the vaulted ceiling, the Universal Declaration of Human Rights – the very one issued at the UN in New York, in both official languages, in 1948. At the time it was held up as proof of the moral superiority of the West over godless Communism. This is the French rendition.

Americans have spent a couple years hating the French for resisting Iraq war hysteria. The French also refused the CIA's torture flights. From London and Dublin alone, hundreds of secret CIA airplanes have apparently been carrying captives and abductees to secret fates in Poland, Romania, Egypt. At least fourteen other nations permitted and facilitated this network. But not one flight stopped anywhere in France.

The French version of Human Rights is, perhaps, to actually mean them. Reason enough to hate France?

As I write, there may be as many as fourteen thousand humans held in US military or CIA prisons, secret or otherwise. In many cases their rights, and they themselves, are nonexistent – in the sense of having been disappeared.

\* \* \*

*From* The Universal Declaration of Human Rights (1948):

Article 6/*Article 6*
Everyone has the right to recognition everywhere as a

person before the law.
*Chacun a le droit à la reconnaissance en tous lieux de sa personnalité juridique.*

❊ ❊ ❊

The day before my flight out of the United States, a hundred or more police lined up before the highrise Federal Building in Portland. Each one was a Black Knight of hard shiny plastic shin-guards and knee and forearm protectors, with black chest and shoulder pads like sci-fi football players. Under helmets and full-face visors they looked like anyone or no one, they were identical athletes of the state, team players, fit and menacing.

I watched them for an hour. In the park across the street, a bannered rumpus declared something about war, something about lies and secrecy. Waving and shouting, standing on curbs and sitting on blankets, the protestors looked skinny (even the fat ones) and vulnerable, as if people. You sensed how easily they could be broken.

The line of athlete-knights stood patient, immobile, ready.

❊ ❊ ❊

On my flight I thought: Dubček will save me.

After Paris would come Prague. And there, I thought, would be the residue of heroism. I would understand from the Czechs how one withstands a propaganda regime, a culture highjacked and reorganized around lying and murder. The Czechs would know how even after twenty years, forty years, one yet *Dubčeks* against it, standing in public and declaring the lie and calling it lie, though skinny and vulnerable.

In 1968 Alexander Dubček, Communist head of state, lifted press censorship and declared open and free elections. "Communism with a human face," was his hopeful program, known as the "Prague Spring," and of course it awoke to Soviet tanks in the streets and a return to repression as usual. Twenty one years later, Gorbachev's *glasnost* and *perestroika* offered such obvious parallels to the obliterated Dubček reforms that the Czech Communist government collapsed of sheer embarrassment just days after the removal of the Berlin Wall, and Dubček himself returned from bureaucratic exile for the transition.

But Prague hardly mentions him. It turns out that Dubček was a Slovak, and his memory must be sought in the former Czechoslovakia's eastern half. I doubt I'll ever go there.

*   *   *

The lie of power is that it is total and will last forever. It wishes to fill the horizon and blot out all other thought. Resistance, at its core, may be simply remembering that this is indeed a lie, an empty pompous boast.

In 1968 Alexander Dubček acknowledged the existence of powers and thoughts from beyond the blotted horizon. This insulted the Soviet empire's overweening statues and deafening speeches. It insulted the dogma which said there was to be no more history – that this was the end of the line and it would last forever. In this the Communists were merely more crude and undisguised than other tyrants – not otherwise different.

Their state terror, too, was not different, only cruder. They threw people out of windows, publicly, to make a point. Ha ha, one imagines them laughing. Says my guide-book:

> On the morning of 10 March 1948 – just days after the communist coup – the body of Jan Masaryk was found in the courtyard of the Cernín Palace. He had fallen to his death from a top-floor bathroom window. Masaryk had been the only son of the respected founder of the Republic, Tomáš Masaryk, and was the only non-communist member of the new government.

There is a weird tradition of political defenestration in the Czech land. This one would be the latest. Just another body dropping from the sky. Ha ha.

Later I found a Prague coffee bar in an old and civilized interior courtyard frequented by students and literary types. I sipped my espresso in a buzz of alien sound, trying hard to think. At the next table three old lions had gathered to talk and argue, papers and books spread around them, hands and arms flying, laughter and sharp retorts. I could not imagine what they knew: how one lives through forty years of lying. Or what it had cost them in insult and complicity. They were grey or balding, pudged out and scruffy, I could see myself in not so many years. But would I know what they knew? What we have flirted with these last six years – what almost engulfed America, the murderous lying militarism that almost, but not quite, tipped us into the full nightmare – (others have had to bear our nightmare for us, in their tens and hundreds of thousands, but we ourselves have been spared) – if it had come upon us, would I have known what these old Czechs knew, how to endure, and remember, and not despair?

The lie of power is that it is eternal and immutable and that there is no point in resisting it. Then it collapses, flowers grow in its cracks, people can breathe again and laugh at dinner, and everyone wonders – what the heck was *that* all about?

❊ ❊ ❊

*From* The Universal Declaration of Human Rights (1948):

Article 1/ *Article premier*
All human beings are born free and equal in dignity and rights. They are endowed with reason and conscience and should act towards one another in a spirit of brotherhood.
*Tous les êtres humains naissent libres et égaux en dignité et en droits. Ils sont doués de raison et de conscience et doivent agir les uns envers les autres dans un esprit de fraternité.*

❊ ❊ ❊

Music is everywhere in Prague. Day and night accordions ply the streets, orchestras swell the gilded palaces, jazz spills out of the clubs.

Music even filled – and defeated – the most famous prison in the Czech land. The Dalibor is a hilltop dungeon-tower built of solid stone in the 1400s. It was designed, of course, to crush its inmates, and by extension to defeat the spirits of all who looked up at it. The usual thing. I saw there the implements of torture displayed for tourists – iron tongs, spikes, collars, boxes, cages. It was hard to think about: *These are real. Actual people used these on other people.* A rack. A wooden bucket for drowning or simulating drowning (what Americans in their sporty way now call "waterboarding").

Yet the tower has been named for its own defeat. Apparently its first prisoner, one Dalibor of Kozojedy, played his violin so sweetly that townsfolk came up the hill and threw him food and cheered. Music invisible, stronger than stone. They had to release him.

Music of any kind, anywhere, is a declaration for beauty and for all fragile things – all things tethered to the body and the breath – breath that says a human name and refuses to let it die soundlessly in secret. That night as I heard Mozart overflowing the swank arches of Prague's "Art Nouveau Hall" I could not stop thinking of it: torture, silence, beauty, victory.

The American regime laughs at attempts to pry information or accountability out of it. The stonewalling that is the universal defense tactic of the Bush war and torture enterprise is, at heart, built of the same stone as the Dalibor. In the end something fragile may defeat it too.

\* \* \*

A flashback. It is the autumn of one of the Bush years, before my foreign sojourn. I am preparing for the writers' group that meets in my home. I am troubled in my spirit, for I have no answers about our darkness. But I have discovered a story about truth.

One morning during the Argentine dictatorship (another regime of murdering generals sustained with the connivance of the CIA) the journalist Rodolfo Walsh left his apartment carrying the result of three months of writing hidden in his jacket. He and his wife had spent the night mimeographing, folding, addressing. He dropped ten copies into the mail. Then he was ambushed by the Argentine secret police and *disappeared.* His body was never found. The letter went to ten destinations. It told the truth about the generals, the *desaparacidos,* the gagging daily menu of official lies and denials.

Within a few years the "Letter to the Generals" was known throughout the Spanish-speaking world. People on every continent could recite passages by heart.

In time the Generals fell. Their leaders somehow escaped prosecution, mocking justice for decades. But during the week in which I did my preparations for my seminar and discovered this famous/obscure writer Walsh, the following news headline appeared: "Generals to face prosecution at last."

\* \* \*

Finding our way in this darkness means finding our way to each other. To tell the truth and the story of the truth. To remember (and declare!) that secrecy and disconnectedness are temporary delusions, that the night of the propaganda-world will be followed by a morning, when toads will be seen again as toads, turds as turds, and lies as lies. Our job is to write our letters – sending them forward in time if need be, or to our own time if listeners can be found. Letters telling the whole truth, as soon as we can figure it out.

Writing and all the arts take place in the public realm, that shared space of discourse, interchange, trade, gift. Capitalist/consumerist societies (like totalitarian ones, but less crude) are always seeking to break down the citizenry into separated individuals, objects of advertising or propaganda, dispirited and powerless. Disconnected people are easily manipulated: In this atomized state, there is no one to challenge lies – there appears to be no public realm, just scattered privacies.

*Extraordinary rendition* and *enhanced interrogation* are the negation of discourse, reason, civilization, humanity. They declare disconnectedness: that what can be done to a person in a secret cell means nothing, can be removed from all context, reduced to a surd. (Surd, that word I learnt from Camus: the absurd thing, the un-meaning.)

This demonic rendition, this reversal of the song of life, is a moral virus working to unmake all other versions, meanings, writings, renditions. This is the blank hopeless dome drawn over us, the cloud of unmaking that drifts from the Pentagon, from the White House, from Guantanamo, from secret prisons in Turkey, Egypt, Poland. A cloud of unmaking not unlike the other invisible pollutions with which we are unmaking ecosystems and climates, prying apart the very molecules of life and breath.

The dark flights crisscross the basilica of our indifference and our permission, their invisible victims drop through our air, the rents and tears in their muscles, tendons, hearts, spirits also rip ours though we are too darkened and too numb to realize it.

We look up. It is a fair day. Do we see them? Each captive is single, alone. More alone than any person can be. Hooded. Deprived. If I try to imagine it, I cannot. Day by day, week by week . . . lost. Who has ever been so lost as this, so abandoned?

There's a gaunt Christ on the cross of Trémalo, the tiny church in rural France near where I am staying. I have just a few more days before returning to America. The broken man looks down on me with a kind of *faux* inscrutability – as if playing along, as if helping us go on pretending to have missed the point. We've only had a couple thousand years to get it – who could blame us?

The church is empty. It is the beginning of summer 2007, and no effective voice in America is raised against torture. Democrats quail and fold, unable to find the boldness of fragility. Progressives speak in soundless vacuums. I try to write in hope, but I cannot see what good it will do.

I wonder if any of us can be saved.

\* \* \*

*From* The Universal Declaration of Human Rights (1948):

> Article 5/**Article 5**
> No one shall be subjected to torture or to cruel, inhuman or degrading treatment or punishment.
> *Nul ne sera soumis à la torture, ni à des peines ou traitements cruels, inhumains ou dégradants.*

# After Rendition . . . Silence

NOVEMBER 2007

If you wonder about the life of a writer, here it is in brief: Be prepared to be ignored.

Starting in May 2007 I sent out the essay "Rendition" into a vacuum of indifference. That we Americans, with our own American hands, were kidnapping, torturing, drowning, abusing and disappearing people at home and around the globe somehow failed to arrest our attention. It is certainly true that revelations were publicly made. The reporting of Dana Priest in the *New York Times*, starting with her June 2004 story about the Bybee/Yoo torture memo, eventually won her a Pulitzer. Hints and premonitions of *extraordinary rendition* were heard long before March of 2005, when the *Times* finally editorialized about it as "one of the biggest nonsecrets in Washington." Of course Abu Ghraib blazoned the torture issue all across the year 2004. Yet the electorate slept through it, dreaming we know not what and returning the torturers to power. A collective shrug – *who cares?*

With the torture came a suite of other domestic violations. If you looked casually over the Bill of Rights, you'd see at least four that were swept off the table like so many broken trinkets, most obviously the Fourth (no search without a warrant). Plus the small matter of *habeas corpus*, the indispensable molecular glue of liberty (Jefferson, on the verge of a rant, tells Madison *habeas corpus* must be "eternal and unremitting"). Nonetheless an American citizen, taken on American soil in 2002, was imprisoned without trial or charge for three and a half years. But again, who cared?

And if perhaps a half-million Iraqis had been killed, and another four million turned into homeless displaced wretches, who cared? America in 2007 was a vast choking muteness, a slow-motion silence. It was like that dream state where you cannot move or speak, though your dream-mind screams for warning, flight, something. We had elected the opposition party to new majorities in both houses of Congress in late 2006 yet . . . nothing . . . could . . . be . . . done. Madness.

"Rendition" was engulfed in this silence. *Poets and Writers* sent it back to me with a tiny preprinted form rejection. *Cabinet* (online and print) declined it. Aiming regionally, I was dismissed by *Northwest Review* and *Oregon Quarterly*. By midsummer I had tried the lovely, lefty national magazine *The Sun*; and (with a sense of grim abandon – why not be rejected by the best?) the classic literaries *Ploughshares* and *North American Review.*

Silence.

❊ ❊ ❊

Someone was waging a war but where was it? A smothering censorship – networks and administration silently collaborating – kept the images from our televisions. We saw no

Iraqis dead or wandering or hungry or despairing. Virtually none. The big numbers sounded bad but what do such numbers mean, really? We didn't know. They came from organizations of foreigners. Maybe they weren't true.

Meanwhile the deaths on our side were somehow covered by the word "heroes," used obsessively. Every soldier a hero. Count on it. Never a Sad Sack or a Bilko or just a clueless kid caught up, used up. *Hero*: a word from comic books, fictional. America saw nothing to put reality into the picture – no combat coverage, no day to day life, no sweat, SNAFUs, catch-22s, mindless violence. And there was never, ever any coverage of dead bodies, caskets or funerals. So each soldier died in a tiny private vortex of pain that seared loved ones and comrades but never the rest of us. We got only polished propaganda eulogies in the local papers.

We were not to know, and we accepted the arrangement. But . . . we knew there was a lot we were not knowing. This had the effect of locking us in our own strange guilty fearful silences. Perfect for empowering the masters.

※ ※ ※

Some time before the election of 2004 I began haunting bookstores with a fierce longing, combing reading lists, searching for that essay, that book, which would help me figure out where we are and what we should be doing. But my reading was often unsatisfactory. Books there were, important ones. Richard Clarke, Stephen Grey. The horrible tale of Mahar Arar, held incommunicado, sent to Syria, tortured, innocent, then coughed back up onto Canadian soil as if "oops" would cover it.

But nothing rang the alarm-bell in the night. In the eerie void I wondered: Were other essays being returned to their authors in silence, other networks tersely rejecting all such unpleasantness?

Or was it simply that the public would not hear?

Barry Lopez's book *Resistance* expressed precisely our desperation: that try as we might, "we cannot tell our people a story that sticks." Where is our voice? What is the "sentence that might break through"? Why did so many persist in believing lies that had been debunked down to the ground – such as those "links" between Saddam and the 9/11 attacks which a full half of the 2004 electorate clung to, even after press-conference admissions to the contrary from President, Vice-President, and Secretary of Defense? What could combat such willful belief in lies, fictions, and fantasies?

Perhaps real fiction could. But Nobel Prize winner José Saramago's novel *Blindness* was so claustrophobic I could not finish it – blindness I knew already, but what then? So I read Derrick Jensen's *The Culture of Make Believe* and found his 900 pages harrowing, his diagnosis exact. Our American habit of ignoring truth is deeply rooted. How deep? I read *Facing West: The Metaphysics of Indian-Hating and Empire-Building* (by Richard Drinnon) to get all the way back to the founding massacre, in 1637, of some seven hundred Pequot men, women, and children burnt alive by the Puritan army in America, in which Indians attempting to escape the encircling soldiery were "entertained at the point of a sword" – as the soldier John Underwood drolly put it. Yes, this is our history, I said to myself – the history we have weirdly replaced by a make-believe version. Recent events suddenly make sense in its flickering light and dreadful smolder. A murderous ideological blindness, with us from the beginning.

Is this too dire? Maybe my little book of essays is unpleasant reading, too. Maybe silence would be better.

Hoping to understand the meaning of state power that metastasizes into killing, militarism, organized lying, I turned to Hannah Arendt, who fled the Nazis and became the philosopher-historian of Nazism and Communism. But I did not have the heart to live in totalitarian darkness for so many pages, so many volumes. Instead I came to cherish her little book *Men In Dark Times,* one-chapter portraits of those who struggled to answer the darkness. Despite the title, not all her subjects are "men" – Arendt admires Rosa Luxemburg's zeal for working people, her irrepressibility. And not all are successes either. Bertolt Brecht created brilliantly humane assaults on Nazism. But Arendt shows how Brecht's meek collaboration with Stalinist terror led him – inevitably – into mediocrity. (There's the cautionary tale for writers: Respond to the lies of power or face something worse, perhaps, than death.)

What I got from Arendt: naming precisely the *kind* of darkness faced, and the specific gestures of courage, truth-telling, and creativity that shined light onto its monstrousness. I have been working hard to see better. I have seen that denial and pretending are universal – pick your century, pick your privilege, your empire. And I see that the American kind of denial is powerful because we are powerful, destructive because when we closed our eyes, we could not see our own values any more.

What else I got from Arendt: that sometimes people need not just the truth, but the *story of* the truth. That was when I stumbled across the story of Rodolfo Walsh, and took heart.

* * *

For several years I struggled with the enormity of this problem, reading, floundering, writing and being unheard. My little essays went out, poems here and there. Occasionally I held a candle at a downtown demonstration – I chose silent, quakerly events, as befitting my temperament and the futility of the gesture. Few of us were in jail but I felt the truth of Arthur Miller's comment on the McCarthy nineteen-fifties: "We were all going slightly crazy trying to be honest and trying to see straight and trying to be safe." Book by book the Iraq debacle was revealed, the house of lies exposed, but public outcry remained stuck in some other land of half-aware anxiety and impotence.

Then at midsummer, rejections accumulating and a mood of resigned abandon coming over me, I realized with a shock – and a laugh – that I had known the answer all along, the reading that would clarify and give voice. Shelley's sonnet "Ozymandias," in just fourteen lines, contained my whole message, my several years of struggling to think and see and find my way, my thousands of words written and canceled, shaped and sent and rejected. Shelley's explosively condensed answer was still potent even after almost two centuries.

It was written during a time of thick darkness in England, a suppurating Regency of corrupt wealth and crushing poverty. Shelley's poem captures Power as that sneering colos-

sus drunk on its own illusion of permanency which we have
come to know too well:

> I met a traveller from an antique land
> Who said: "Two vast and trunkless legs of stone
> Stand in the desert. Near them on the sand,
> Half sunk, a shattered visage lies, whose frown
> And wrinkled lip and sneer of cold command
> Tell that its sculptor well those passions read
> Which yet survive, stamped on these lifeless things,
> The hand that mocked them and the heart that fed.
> And on the pedestal these words appear:
> 'My name is Ozymandias, King of Kings:
> Look on my works, ye mighty, and despair!'
> Nothing beside remains. Round the decay
> Of that colossal wreck, boundless and bare,
> The lone and level sands stretch far away."

In the end, it is simple fact of ongoing of life in the daylight
world that mocks the sneering face, the oval-office swagger,
the scorn for decency. It cannot have been easy for Shelley
to sustain this faith. Nor is it for us. I confess I did not read
the entire chain of excellent tomes about Iraq and its politics that appeared over the last several years – so detailed, so
factual, so awful. Really the facts were glaringly obvious if
you didn't deny them; I think I was groping for the *meaning*
of the facts. The story of the truth. Strange that I found it in
something so brief and antique as a sonnet, written before
Iraq (per se) even existed.

Yet I guess it should not surprise us that, after all, poetry saves best. Poetry has no expiration date. Most nonfiction – even most novels – fade quickly. Built of quotidian chaff and controversy, they fail to outlive their makers. What unaging magic brings a book to life a decade or a century later? *Imagination.* Language and conception that somehow transform the yellowing misery of the passing moment into the evergreen miracle, the unforgettable reflection of something deeper, truer. Carolyn Forché's poems in *The Country Between Us* described a now-vanished dictatorship, yet their precise record of horror remains bright and all but unbearably current. Adrienne Rich's *Atlas of the Difficult World* answered the first Bush and the first Gulf War with twenty-three pages of heartbreaking clarity. It still answers.

At length I found even nonfiction that lifts us from the labyrinth of the moment: Rebecca Solnit's *Hope in the Dark,* the true and lasting account of our time. Books like this will remain precious and lifegiving when Bush and Cheney have become mere heads on stakes in the shuddering collective memory of our nation.

❊ ❊ ❊

On the fifteenth day of November, 2007, a Congressperson stood in the well and, with Patrick Henry clarity, denounced an administration of "Big Brother" megalomania. That's happened before, but this time it got on the evening news. Something has begun to shift. Earlier that month, a presidential candidate stood for something in the Senate and defeated the administration's attempt to bury its past violations of the First Amendment. And this week – I write in the present, wondering at meanings – Democrats actually passed an Iraq funding bill that required a pullout (then almost immediately faltered and withdrew it, illustrating again the complicity of Democrats in this Republican catastrophe).

All this is merely the dust of history, the small grit of how things happened and didn't happen. Next week more grit will blow. But there is, at long last, something in the wind. The weird silence is cracking, and moments of effectual action are starting to be seen, even from these dithering and pathetic Democrats. Alas, Americans won't get the impeachment trial they need, the needed inoculation against future tyranny: Our children will face it again sooner, not later, because we wouldn't. But for now, the lurking parafascism of military-industrial Americanism seems to be done. For the moment I feel less crazy, less trapped in doublethink and pretending – though also more chastened about the darkness of human history, its ability to go terribly wrong at any moment. Being an American offers no insurance against that.

In September of this year, another book in the archipelago of truth appeared: *The Administration of Torture: A Documentary Record from Washington to Abu Ghraib and Beyond*, by Jameel Jaffer and Amrit Singh. And in October, a big movie with big stars that used (up?) my unread and unknown title: *Rendition*.

Perhaps my trying-so-hard essay wasn't needed. America went forward without it. Or maybe it will serve in retrospect as a marker, like what you see in towns that have been flooded: a muddy line on a wall. Perhaps a scrawled message – *We were here. This is how high it got.*

# And after Silence?

Satire.

According to the wisdom of editors, my "Rendition" material didn't work. Played as tragedy, perhaps, the killing and the lying were too much for anyone. Evidently I was so flabbergasted and heartsick, I could only run head-foremost, repeatedly, into the same bloody brick wall. Wham. Wham. Wham.

I do know better. My motto (from Emily Dickinson): *Tell all the truth, but tell it slant*. Find a sly angle, a flip. Frontal assaults? Not so much. I thought that brick wall was hard. But as the old vaudevillians say: "Hard? Now *comedy* – that's hard!"

What did work: mockery. Laughter. Stephen Colbert and Jon Stewart. Molly Ivins.

With material provided daily by a White House – a *conservative party* so achingly spendthrift and heedless of the past – so hypocritical, deadly, greedy, and so very inept – satire was really the only possible way to go. With Godly lies and Christian slaughter everywhere, with Mayberry Machiavellis and pious criminals heading to prison, what else? I ought to have been saying "Thank you!" every writing day of my life.

* * *

The greatest satirist of the last millennium or two wrote his own surprisingly blunt epitaph:

> Here lies Jonathan Swift, where fierce indignation no longer lacerates his breast.

Jonathan Swift was enraged not only by the general feebleness of human nature (often enough his target), but by the particular self-serving brutality of British rule in Ireland and the bourgeois prigs that cashed in on it in England. But a glimpse of Swift's rage is also, if you think about it, a glimpse of his genius in ever finding a slant that would excoriate while never failing to amuse; in always sustaining his wit and verve despite the heart-grasping loathsomeness of the governing murder and misrule from which he, too, gained his living (as a privileged Englishman in Ireland, ultimately Dean of St. Patrick's). *Oh, Gulliver-giants and little Lilliputians, talking horses and floating islands. Haw! Haw! Haw! Really my dear Doctor Swift.* "A Modest Proposal!" *Oh my dear how droll.*

No better answer to the immiseration of the many for the enrichment of the few was ever written. No better rebuke to tyrants, hereditary or elected.

I think Jon Stewart and Stephen Colbert are *modest proposaling* us nightly. There's a reason they have a following in the millions – perhaps the hopefullest sign in all this miserable mess. Every laugh, in each and every living room, is a fresh antidote to shouting-at-the-TV, a fresh inoculation against despairing and giving in to the propaganda machine. Laughter is music without the notes, spontaneous acknowledgement of a shared reality that makes the fantasies of our rulers frankly absurd.

The torturers have their gags. And we have ours.

\* \* \*

Herewith: a brief list of as-yet unused titles. Birds waiting to be flipped. Farts saved for future elevator moments with Republican True-Believers. Unwritten *bon mots*, retorts, wise-cracks, raspberries, aperçus, limericks, fablieux, Playboy jokes. Things to read to Ashcroft while his minion puts a sheet over the (gasp) *nude* statue. To Bush if you should find yourself in a receiving line. To Cheney if you should find yourself chained to an adjacent stalagmite in Hell.

Modest essays, I would think – if they ever get written. Just right for those end-of-article-spaces in a *Readers Digest* of some alternate universe, where Grampa could call out, *Here – listen to this one . . .* And everyone would wonder – Now, who in the world would have voted for such people?

Baking hints from Condi
Andover Cowboy Songs
Waterboarding *vs.* Baptism: You Be the Judge
January 18, 2009: Bush's Last Dry Day
Ten Steps to a Slimmed-Down Bill of Rights
Habeas Corpus? *The UnAmerican "Right" with the
UnAmerican Name*

It's Not Torture if You're Not Dead!
The Only Three Bible Verses You Need to Know
It's Not Illegal if the President Does it . . . *because He's the President!*
We've Put Your Rights Away to Keep Them Safe
It Feels Warmer but Trust Me It Isn't
Don't Tell Me Americans Aren't Prospering – *they're fatter than ever!*

I did get one or two written. They follow.

# Lacking the Subjunctive

The subjunctive is disappearing from English.

Maybe this is not the biggest news of a decade in which four-tenths of the Bill of Rights also disappeared, along with half the value of your house and most of the Arctic. Nonetheless . . . Some people watch birds, some grow vegetables, others send money to as-yet-undisgraced televangelists (when they can find them). Me, I notice words. I can't help it. They have their seasons, too.

Subjunctives express possibilities, projecting imagined states that do not (yet) exist. A special form for fantasy and desire! Verbal playground, box of sweets, dreamland – you'd think we could hardly stay away from it. But the subjunctive survives only in a few stock phrases, like "If it please (not *pleases*) the court" and "God bless (not *blesses)* America." Regular folks don't construct subjunctives fresh as they speak any more. I keep track – even highly-educated language-users are drifting this way, and of course it's way too late for television journalists, selected for hairful obedience. "If the President was serious, he'd . . ." they say, or "If I was rich . . ." That *were* thing (the normal subjunctive) is vanishing. The recent book title of unconvicted maybe-murderer O.J. Simpson is disturbingly *off* (like everything about him) precisely here, in its cross-threaded verb: *If I Did It.* It's not a subjunctive, though it ought to be ("Had I done it" or even "Were I to have done it"). In pretending to pretend he believes we believe he didn't do it, O.J. gets lost in the difference between reality and imagination (or lie). It's the familiar note of our messed-up little decade. Anything to sell a book. Or a war.

In modern English the subjunctive mood is melting back into the indicative mood, which is problematic since indicatives "indicate" what *is*, plain and simple. (A "mood" of course is not a verb tense but a separate form within the tense. English used to have three moods: indicative, imperative, subjunctive.) So – lacking the subjunctive – where does *maybeing* go? Where's the praying and dreaming mood? And how do we register the difference between what *is* and what *might be*?

Here's a telling example. When we sing "America, America,/God shed his grace on thee," we seem to be expressing a patriotic faith that the Divinity has "shed his grace" particularly on us. But the next line revises that notion: "And crown thy good with brotherhood/from sea to shining sea." Why not "crowned" – to go with "shed"? Because both verbs are subjunctive, of course. It's the equivalent of saying "May God shed his grace on thee and may God crown thee with brotherhood." The anthem is a prayer for grace and brotherhood, not a declaration that they're already here. But if you listen, more than half the singers on any occasion just say "crowned," as if God had already done it. Which turns the anthem into a cheer: Yay! God loves us best!

A great divide separates those who pray the prayer from those who cheer the cheer. Some work to make it more true – that blessing and brotherhood should be ever more real among us. Others just shout – Hooray for our side! No criticism allowed.

※ ※ ※

Subjunctives in languages around the world are as numerous and mysterious as subatomic particles. Linguists have found perhaps sixteen different kinds – sixteen ways to pray, imagine, doubt, and fancy! You might know some of these subjunctive flavors if you studied Greek or Latin. I didn't – but the feel of their names is mouth-candy:

| | |
|---|---|
| cohortative | dubitative |
| eventive | hypothetical |
| jussive | imperative |
| interrogative | negative |
| optative | potential |
| presumptive | volative |
| admirative | inferential |

Language is ever-changing and though the subjunctive in English may be on its way out, I'm not worried. If the subjunctive die, it will rise again. I predict that English will drop the subjunctive mood but replace it by a flurry of new subjunctive-like verbs. (If imaginary science has sci-fi, why can't imaginary grammar have gra-fi?) Empires will fall, sea levels rise, folks wonder what those idiots at the beginning of the twenty-first century were thinking. They will be sulky. Overstressed. Their verbs will be *extremely* moody.

\* \* \*

Herewith, my semi-fictional forecast:

**The "Indicative" will become the "Credulative."** People will believe whatever they are told. That's what TV is for. This has already come to pass. And soon we will realize that the Credulative mood has been joined by these new sub-junctive-replacement moods:

**The Deniative** – for things that one wishes did not exist. Information in the Deniative simply cannot stay in the American mind (or mind-replacement). Linguists will find that *anything contradicting current propaganda* has roughly the half-life of a chocolate lepton. Even when you see it, you can't see it.

**The Exploitional** – used for corporate public relations. This happy mood is for conveying to consumers (formerly called "citizens") the nice things that Exxon is doing for the world, or how many ways Monsanto has of making you happy.

**The Devouratory** - for corporate *internal* memos only. When the indicative is no longer trustworthy, corporate raiders need some way to communicate actuality to each other. Specifically, what to take and how to take it.

**The Perfunctive** – mainly used 1990-2020 – by politicians pretending to do something about earth-warming, constitu-tion-abandoning, and the like.

**The Suppository** – used to implant suggestions without seeming to do so. A favorite of advertisers and politicians ever since Henry II asked, "Will no one rid me of this troublesome priest?" Hillary: "Gee, candidates sometimes get assassinated in June . . ." Richard Nixon (after mentioning a particularly heinous tactic): "But it would be *wrong,* that's for sure! Heh, heh."

**The Remorsative** – for things too painful to think about but too awful to forget. This mood will spread out from country-western music to become the most potent emotive force in the language, verbally identified by a distinctive western twang and a twisting of the hands, like Lassie's mom with a dishtowel. Journalists however will never use it, being stuck in pretend-indicative (see Credulative) and well-paid (see Devouratory).

**The Perhaptic** – wishful thinking in the sense of "perhaps what is clearly inevitable will be averted in some inconceivable way" – a verb form for doing the same thing over and over again, while hoping for different results.

**The Opt-out-ative** – for wishing to leave the whole mess and go to a different planet, sphere, or plane of consciousness.

\* \* \*

The drift of our verbs toward these strange new forms is already influencing everyday politics. It's easy to see when you know what to look for. Rev. Jeremiah Wright, briefly famous as "Barack Obama's pastor," committed the political sin of speaking religious truth that conflicts with Americanism, our reigning propaganda religion. The religious truism Wright voiced was simply this: Your nation isn't God:

> God damn America for as long as she acts like she is
> God and she is supreme.

As an urgent request to the Almighty, it's one of those subjunctives: God *damn* (not the indicative God *damns* or *damned*). And it is strong language, naughty like cursing – unless meant in the theological sense, which it clearly is. In fact, Wright preaches the basic Judeo-Christian idea that God's people do not worship creatures – not even big powerful institutional ones – not Pharaohs nor Babylons, not Presidents nor even Americas. People of uncorrupted faith worship the Creator instead, who erects a standard of justice and mercy and love that can challenge the popular bigotries of the moment (like jingoistic country-worship on CNN and Fox). Idolaters of country are, by definition, to be damned. Simple.

But no one heard the subjunctive. The public misheard it the same way they mishear that patriotic "God crown[ed] thy good with brotherhood . . . ," mistaking a prayed imaginative possibility as one of simple indication.

Meanwhile, a Texas televangelist (whom the Republican presidential candidate had very publicly embraced) known as Rev. Hagee was declaring that God *had already* damned America, or at least parts of it. He actually did use the indicative. He told a radio interviewer on a national show, "Hurricane Katrina was, in fact, the judgment of God against the city of New Orleans." Elsewhere he stated repeatedly that God had indicatively *cursed* America (his word).

A weird silence surrounded it. Hagee's statement was mentioned once in the news, then dropped. Yet the Rev.

Wright's utterance dominated coverage on CNN and other stations for a week or more – every time I looked up at a gym or a tavern, there'd be a panel of "experts" explaining again why, how, maybe, bad, terrible. But Hagee's statements? One news story and . . . blink. Gone. As if they were never heard.

I propose a grammar-fictional explanation: The Hagee episode illustrates the emerging *deniative mood,* wherein inconvenient indicative statements are silently vaporized. The last eight years have surely illustrated this developing mental habit. There is no torture, corruption, or malfeasance that can't be *deniatived.*

When Hagee spoke in the deniative, his audience knew exactly what to do: forget about it.

✳ ✳ ✳

A last gra-fi prediction. Under the stressful conditions of the next thousand years, verb tenses themselves will have to change. They will follow the moods into a twilight of quasi-reality. Instead of *present tense, past tense, future tense* there will be:

> Relatively Tense
> Extremely Tense
> Too Tense to Cope At All

Hagee spoke in the Too Tense. It helped with the vaporizing.

And the "perfect tenses" must certainly be doomed – how could they be viable once the temperature hits 100 degrees? The three we currently know (*present perfect, future perfect, past perfect*) will miserabilize into two:

The Somewhat Imperfect
and
The Totally Screwed

(*"Past Perfect"* will be expressible only indirectly, via the Remorsative.)

\* \* \*

What happens when the indicative and the subjunctive run together? When both love of truth and healthy imagining vanish, what's left is mere pretense – pretending to believe what you know damn well isn't true. (Or ought to know!) Pretense is the fog-zone between the really *imagined* and the really *real*. It's neither. It's what has governed us for the last eight years.

Pretense is what allows the "real" to be transformed into the back-door subjunctive, as when our Chief Executive characterized those annoying Iraq warnings of career experts at CIA and State Department as . . . "just a guess." It's a marvelous fantasy world we then get to live in – the fog of pretense illuminated by the glow of money and the reddish hue of other people's suffering.

Pleasant, at least until consequences start dropping on our dreaming heads, like cartoon anvils of real-life iron.

# *Threat Level: TEAL*

UNDER-REPORTED STORIES OF 2004

A Freedom of Information Act request has revealed that just days before his resignation in late 2004, Homeland Security Czar Tom Ridge announced a new 36-color Threat Level Scale. At the same press conference, Ridge also announced a change of title from Czar to Headmaster, effective immediately.

"As you can see, the new colors allow us to exactly calibrate threats and risks, which will enable loyal Americans to go about their daily business while also adopting the appropriate posture, or postures, of risk-aversion, vigilance, and generalized anxiety," said the newly-designated Headmaster.

The multicolored Threat Levels were displayed on a pie-chart. Homeland Security Agents claimed this new arrangement had "already revealed actionable intelligence" based on previously unnoticed complementarities between colors on opposite sides of the wheel; for instance, between Turquoise (denoting "moderate evildoing assisted by small-bore weapons easily hidden in bulky winter or late-fall garments, which are sold in the summer now so really that only leaves out spring") and its opposite Mildly-Hot Pink ("naughtiness, high spirits and possible randiness associated with the first really dry, sunny day we've had since last October, since April was so wet").

The color relations, referred to as "Seasonal Terror Appositionals" by CIA analysts wearing conservative and, it must be said, beautifully tailored blue blazers, were characterized as strong confirmation of the new system. "Coincidence? I think Not!" declared the Headmaster's aide, a tall young man known at the time only as Toby (his title, it was later revealed, had been "Boys Vice Principal").

Headmaster Ridge explained that the current threat level was "Teal," positioned below Aubergine but above Eggplant and slightly to the left of Millet. "I feel better about this. Toby feels better. And, may I say, America feels better," he said, indicating the day's color with a pointer. "America will not be bullied by evildoers in shapeless earth-toned garments!"

After the announcement, staff members reportedly set up easels displaying pencil and ink-wash sketches for the Homeland Security Department's planned new uniforms, which showed black-leather accents and "very retro" Sam-Browne straps. Questioned sharply by a reporter from *GQ*, Ridge replied only that he was changing his title back to Czar, then to Master of Revels, then back to Tsar, in order to get to Kevin Bacon in three moves.

Sources have independently corroborated what happened next. Shouts were heard from the back of the room, "It's going to Aubergine! Aubergine!" and reporters scattered in panic, knocking over the easels and spoiling the festive unveiling. A distraught Toby was heard to say into an open mike, "But I'm not giving up the Eisenhower jackets!"

The later appointment of Michael Chertoff to Ridge's vacated position was said by experienced White House fashion sources to be largely "in keeping with the kicky new Russian look."

Within hours of the color-chart unveiling fiasco, bloggers revealed that a young Bacon had once auditioned for the role of medieval Cossack terrorizer Taras Bulba in a since-forgotten Broadway musical, wearing a daring costume of burnt orange and crimson in an attractive yet masculine off-the-shoulder pillaging-cape-cum-rain-poncho. Chertoff is said to be considering it.

## The Real Fake

Here's my picture of Ronald Reagan astride his horse. He's on his ranch, where he was famous for riding and clearing brush and generally cowboying it up. Though it's a "ranch" only in the sense of a lot of acreage with a view, on a million-dollar hilltop by the Pacific Ocean.

And he's in jodhpurs.

*Jodhpurs?*

Does any of this say "cowboy," for real? Of course not. Yet, right after Reagan's death came the commemorative stamp: rugged-handsome grin, cowboy hat. "He was so real, so absolutely real" said the inevitable obituary quote. People truly thought this guy was an authentic brush-grubbing western man's-man. They think so still. He played "Reagan" so convincingly that contradicting evidence never made the slightest difference. He looked the part. That was the reality.

Now here's George W. Bush, the Yaley cowboy – an obvious phony, imitating his predecessor phony by pretending (what else) to clear brush. On another "ranch" devoid of cattle. To my eye he seemed a small man shielding his sense of inadequacy with a tough-guy act. But for most of the electorate he remained the real man, the guy you'd like to drink a beer with.

Why does the public so adore a really good fake?

❧ ❧ ❧

So I wondered as I took a wet spring walk in the Coast Range. I had a cabin for three days, a little brook, a little time.

"Wondered" might be too pale a word. *Seethed*, probably. It's my old bugaboo, fakery and lying and the world opening its big whorey arms to them . . . Gah. This is not a good mind to carry on a walk. Honestly, I get so tired of myself. Up I went along a mud trail dripping bleeding-heart and sprouting trillium beneath second-growth alder. Somewhere on the ridgeline stood remnant firs, and I'd rage up there too when I found them.

A paradoxical whoosh – like helicopters six inches away – buzzed me almost off my feet, a blur heading straight downslope past my head and then and up, up, maybe two hundred feet into the spring-grey sky, a furious speck that immediately *whirred* back down the hillside and *swooped* back up again, three times in all, and I couldn't tell if the hummingbird was trying to run me off or if I had simply witnessed a performance pointed elsewhere. Such noise! Such height! I might have been seeing with hummy eyes, androgynously – first scared, then romanced.

He angled toward me, gorget shimmering crimson. I was his.

Yet it was all display, wasn't it? A big show to scare off rival males and attract mates. The perplexing thing about this "sexual selection," as Darwin called it, is that while the observing female assesses displaying males in order to identify a better boyfriend, she's no gene decoder and in place of measuring actual fitness, she has to read something that *stands for* fitness. Whirring in this case. And flashy appearance and really good singing.

Wait – Isn't that exactly what every girl's mother warns against?

To no avail. The males put on the biggest strut they can and hope it convinces. I'm beautiful! I sing gorgeously! I'm the baddest prettiest singiest thing in all the treetops in the land-i-o!! They're *acting* their maleness.

In one of his earlier books, biologist Stephen Jay Gould depicts the skeleton of the now-extinct Irish Elk, with a rack of antlers twelve feet across. Gould speculates about the point at which this elk's *symbolic* fitness might have become too much for its *actual* fitness to bear. All that antler, just to impress the girls . . . and the boys. Gould, like most contemporary students of animal life, is pretty clear that the point of armament like this is not (as early Darwinists assumed) to *use* it – the point is to be so impressive the other guy just goes away and leaves you to mate in peace. A preemptive masculine bluff. Visual whirring.

But when the bluff fails, it's bad – possibility of wounds or worse. Sometimes you see skeletons of bucks, antlers fatally tangled, who starved to death.

* * *

So I got to thinking about alpha-maleness. Leadership, followership. Buckhood, that burden my gender bears.

Myself, I'm alpha only in very limited contexts. Mostly I'm in some other alphabet altogether, an opportunist going my own way, cocky indeed, but always more coyote than cock of the walk. So I see both display and aggression mostly from the outside. Once however . . .

"Oates, I want you to look more like a Climbing Instructor." That was Robin, my mentor and chieftain, ten years senior, honcho of a troubled-youth outdoor program in the Sierras. We took the boys (and later, girls) rock climbing, scared them, dragged them on twelve-day mountaineering exploits. "But I'm not a very good climber," I retorted. "You're good enough to keep them safe." That part was true.

Robin handed me the multiple nylon slings known (unironically) as a "rack," hung gorgeously with purple and yellow and red runners and gleaming carabiners and metallic doodads. You wore it across one shoulder. "Walk across the base camp every morning as you head out to set up the rock. Rattle around. Look the part." He sensed my horror – Inauthenticity. Vulgar display. "It's not for you. It's for the boys. Just do it."

I did. It worked. No one cared about my existential authenticity. I ching-chinged confidently across the camp each morning, roped and bandoliered. And when I had a fourteen- or sixteen-year-old on the face of our granite dome, he did what I said. There wasn't any backtalk because a) he was scared, and b) I seemed to know what I was doing.

To a surprising extent, leadership is bluffing. Reality got nothin' to do with it.

Well, I guess it helped that I'm vigilant and cautious and

a good teacher. No fear of heights. And I liked clambering around on our pretty-big granite. Still – just looking good will usually get you the part.

\* \* \*

All's fair in love and war, and alpha-males know this instinctively. Look big, you are big. Usually, no one has the means of measuring anything more precisely.

Did I say *big*? You've probably heard that the human branch of the primate family has (by far) the biggest penis. Evolutionary explanations for this usually follow that Darwinian concept of sexual selection. Once females begin to select for a trait, it's trapped in a one-way process of intensification – a positive feedback cycle. In this case we're up on two legs and there it is, the selectable, delectable emblem of maleness. No wonder we obsess about it. Darwin, in *Origin of Species,* explained brilliantly how such a process worked (long before the word "feedback" existed). End result: bright gorgets, spectacular racks and songs, and (if you're lucky) pendulous penes. But let's remember, these are symbols – even the latter example! They *stand for* fitness.

So what is "really" male? Whatever is admired as such. Any selected portrayal of maleness gets copied into the next generation's genes. Appearance and reality are not, in other words, so neatly separated. If you're *acting* maleness, then it's all about show, not authenticity. In the middle ages, the show could include gigantic penis-simulacra – like the docent-embarrassing codpiece in that Holbein painting, the green one, of a poker-proud aristocratic boy. He whirrs and struts from centuries away.

What's maler than male? The same, only more so. If you feel admired, then you are admirable, and (thinking practically here, since this is about reproductive fitness) this feeling can only help get your maleness up and running.

Whoever plays the part has the part. And vice versa.

* * *

Umberto Eco tried to make sense of the attraction to really good fakes as if it were an especially American trait. The various Disneylands. Museum dioramas. Marinelands. Las Vegas. And especially those bits of borrowed Europeanry re-presented in a heightened fashion – like the *stained glass* version of Da Vinci's "Last Supper" at Glendale, California's Forest Lawn Cemetery . . . which the hushed narrator will tell you *was produced by a Lost Art of stained-glass-making!* I went there on school field trips more than once. The gigantic "David" stood close by – rather hypnotizing to me for reasons which became obvious later – a perfect reproduction although of course he is demurely fig-leafed. The real thing, improved; Eco called it *hyperreality*. Eco finds that "the American imagination demands the real thing and, to attain it, must fabricate the absolute fake." In an America that lacks deep history, the fake satisfies in a way the merely real never does. We invest it with "kitsch reverence."

Eco's wry commentary is a perfect antidote for those unavoidable moments of Disneyfication lurking around too many American corners. But really I wonder if he wasn't missing something in the larger frame. Where's the border line between real and fake, after all? If you play it convincingly, aren't you really it? A lot about male display seems like hyperreality. Exaggeration, pretense. Gilding that lily. And male hyperreality is part of a much larger natural pattern: Nature fakes stuff all the time. Flowers hoodwink horny insects. Blue jays make hawk-screeches to edge out competitors. Real bluffs or fake realities? And the sheer excess of orchids, bower birds, and a million other critters surely crosses over to the hyper-real. Whatever fakery is, it's no less natural than authenticity.

Yet I carry a deep uncritical preference for something I register as "real." I hate lying with a nearly unhinged fervency (having done a lot of it myself). But I wonder at my assumptions. If I can't see any clear dividing line between the mere performance and the real thing, then I'm a bit lost.

This is a mirrory world, and it seems to want clever looking, not simplicity.

※ ※ ※

I conclude (somewhat reluctantly) that masculinity – and in a masculinist culture, leadership – are largely bluff. A matter of skilled acting and ostentatious posturing. Consider the strategic episode often cited as Ronald Reagan's triumph: Crushing The Soviet Union Through The "Space-Based Missile Defense" Program (hero-worshipping capitals recommended). Reagan pushed through a program that gobbled up billions of real dollars even as the world mocked it as a "Star Wars" delusion. Many a test was faked, many a press-release released.

But it didn't work then and – even after decades of technical advances – still doesn't. At least, not in the conventional sense of "working." (We'll see what other sense that leaves in a minute.)

I was thirty-something, never a warrior, and a bit shy about math when Alpha-Reagan (as I think of him) introduced Star Wars. But ten minutes with the back of an envelope were all I needed to see its uselessness. Here's the logic. Both sides had about 25,000 nuclear warheads. Presume that most of the Soviets' were aimed at the biggest US cities (for deterrence) and – to make it a very conservative thought-experiment – not aimed at the missile-defense system. And let's indulge conservatism further and stipulate Reagan's full fantasy: an *inconceivably good* Star Wars system, capable of shooting down, say, 90% of its targets.

Here they come, 20,000 warheads launched at US cities (subtracting five thousand targeted elsewhere). Wait, let's be reality-based at least for the Evil Empire: Stipulate that *only half* the Soviet thundersticks get off the ground – the rest are left venting in alcoholic totalitarian incompetence. So 10,000 missiles have lifted off toward the top one hundred US cities – 100 missiles each, arcing toward New York, Los Angeles, Chicago, Dallas, Philadelphia, Houston, Miami, Washington, Atlanta, Detroit, Boston, SF, Phoenix, Riverside/Orange County, Seattle, Minneapolis, San Diego, St. Louis, Tampa, Baltimore, Denver, Pittsburgh, Portland, Cleveland, Cincinnati . . . that makes just the top twenty-five: the list goes on to Chattanooga, Tennessee, our Census Bureau's one-hundredth largest metropolitan area.

After Star Wars eliminates 90% of them (*Yay!*) . . . the Soviets still score 10 nuclear explosions per city. Is this a credible deterrent?

Call it the jodhpur defense. It makes no sense.

Stack the deck further in Star War's favor. What if the Soviets get only a *quarter* off the ground, and if only a *quarter* of those actually turn out to be capable of exploding – leaving merely 1,225 truly operational missiles to be winnowed by this fantastically good missile-defense system? Result: "just" one nuke or so per city (1.22 on average). Each about fifty times the size of the Hiroshima explosion. Times a hundred cities. Is this a credible defense?

Pretty-good defense is pointless. With nuclear weapons, defense must be virtually perfect. Even ninety percent efficiency isn't good enough! This is why only mutual deterrence really works, as history has shown and as I assume any number of Pentagon experts must have pointed out. But apparently this reality-based calculus didn't matter. Reagan's eyes glistened whenever he spoke in public about his utopian, technological, impossible solution. And we spent billions. *On what*, I would rant over beers to my friends. *On what?*

Apparently, on a bluff. Because the really disturbing, weirdly pleasing, and truly farcical outcome seems to have been – that the Soviet generalship was equally deluded and starry-eyed. *They believed it.* If Alpha-Reagan's deficit-funded military largess really "spent the Soviets" into their collapse – a big if – then this is how: One big posing puff-adder outpuffed the other. This makes a damn good tale, because it makes no sense – except in illustrating the way the world actually works. Cockalooey.

Reality had nothin' to do with it. Not that it mattered.

Bluffing can be dangerous, though. Poor strutting George

W. Bush (Beta-Reagan) believed a bluff himself – Saddam Hussein's, pretending to have big missiles – with disastrous results for both. Apparently bluffing is no good if your opponent doesn't behave rationally (those tangled bucks come to mind . . .).

And of course, there are still those bills to pay. Twenty-five years later, a big chunk of our national debt pays for Reagan's pretend defense. Most of the rest is for Bush's disastrous swaggering. Real consequences do have a way of showing up.

\* \* \*

Might as well laugh. Join the hyenas, the baying coyotes, the laugh-track millions at their sit-coms. Better to laugh it off than gravel my guts over truth and authenticity. And anyway, I wonder if the public on some level actually recognizes male pretending all too well. Maybe the public reads Reagan and Bush as "authentic" because insecurity, hidden behind aggression and pretense, is so many men's everyday reality. Maybe a lot of women, too, have found that's what you have to settle for – prop up – and go along with. Maybe our feeble cowboy-pretender presidents were after all the perfect mirror of a culture trying to sustain an illusory image of the Authoritative Man.

Doubts about these men there are, but they must never be expressed, not even whispered. (What happens if our men have to admit their meagerness? Will they cease to function, go limp? Will all our infallible preachers, angry talk-show hosts, bellowing football coaches, thuggy marines, cocksure Defense Secretaries, beer-drinking working stiffs . . .

suddenly go un-stiff? Will we thus be fatherless, leaderless, unprotected before the awful world?)

I have my own doubts. I wonder how much of what we call "culture" is really a group effort to keep our men's imaginative lives uncluttered enough that they can harden and rise to the moment of generation. Are we really driven by a fearful biological imperative, based on the simple fact that sex is first of all a mental act, and if the mind isn't right the body will not follow? The female hummer had *better* settle for one vainglorious show-off or another. And we (as a species) cannot go unfucked for long and still have a future, either. So we let these men fuck us every way they want, and call it manly. It's a terrible bargain.

Or a funny one. But don't get caught laughing – it spoils the mood.

# When Denial Is Public Policy
SEPTEMBER 2007

One sunny afternoon some years ago, I was picked up at our Hawthorne Boulevard Starbucks. A goodlooking fellow caught me glancing at him from my window seat and soon followed me out the door toward . . . what? My home was just blocks away. He whispered things unrestrained, aggressive. I admit the attention was flattering: I had recently become single again. But this . . . Yipes!

I detoured us toward a park bench for some conversation instead of instant sex. Here it got weirder. He revealed that he was a long-time resident in the local Baptist Church's "ex-gay ministry," located in a Victorian mansion visible from the Starbucks window. "So what the heck are you doing?" I asked. He shook his head, wordless, unable to disown his sexuality or disown his disapproval of it. He was stuck in a lie, and he ended up roaming around in a predatory way that dishonored him and me both.

Some ministry.

A short while later, the Portland newspaper's conservative commentator ran an admiring series about this very program, uncritically repeating stories of "deliverance from gayness" and capping them with the tale of prominent ex-gay leader John Paulk, then heading "Exodus International" and married to a woman after years as, apparently, a real flamer.

But one's basic sexuality is not all that malleable. Virtually no gay men actually change, and "ex-gay" programs do little but heap self-loathing on top of already-wounded psyches. In fact, a few years before my sexy, creepy near-adventure, two of Exodus International's "ex-gay" co-founders hooked up, quit the organization, and held a commitment ceremony. John Paulk? Photographed socializing in a D.C. gay bar, quite a while after his "marriage."

But the newspaper puff-piece offered little of this larger, more doubtful reality. It was a sadly familiar conservative performance, telling a carefully selected morsel of the truth and suppressing the rest.

\* \* \*

Making the real world vanish in a puff of belief: That – sadly – is what Republicanism has been turned into by fervent hacks and archconservative politicians, like Senator Larry Craig of Idaho, whose scandal toward the end of the Bush years brought my little misadventure back to mind. Since even salacious headlines fade fast, I'll just say that the Senator was caught soliciting sex in a Minneapolis airport men's room, and subsequently convicted (with a guilty plea). His plaintive "I'm not gay" is the part of his resignation speech we all remember best.

My point is not just the hypocrisy. Of course Sen. Craig had voted consistently to deny gay people marriage rights or even civil rights protections in their jobs – apparently while cruising for gay sex in secret. Of course gay Christians are entitled to settle their consciences however they choose. Denial is a human failing, and as such deserves compassion.

But when denial moves from being a *private* vice to being *public* policy, it damages and dishonors all of us. A perfect example unfolded here in the Northwest just preceding the bathroom *contretemps*, when Craig and other Republican senators attempted to make another part of our reality vanish.

The Fish Passage Center, located in Portland, provides technical services to the agencies which manage the Columbia River's salmon. The FPC counts adult salmon coming upstream and smolts (hatchlings) coming down. It monitors water conditions and provides timely data as well as historical comparisons to decision-makers in Washington and scientists in the field.

Its only purpose is to provide information about the state of salmon in the river. But since the state of salmon is dire, the FPC quite often brings bad news – especially bad news for then-Senator Craig's timber- and power-industry supporters, who would rather not admit that restoration plans are not working and might need an expensive upgrade. So the Senator arranged to make the FPC vanish. With his seniority and the clout of a Republican majority, he personally inserted language into a bill to cancel its funding in 2005. (Fortunately, the 9th Circuit Court of Appeals undid the defunding a year later.)

In this kill-the-messenger response, Sen. Craig merely facilitated Republican policies of dishonesty and denial that have so deeply marred our nation and our world: Global warming is a hoax . . . Saddam is behind 9/11 . . . Iraq's weapons of mass destruction require a war . . . Abstinence-only doctrine must replace sex education . . . and so on. Sen. Craig had been a reliable vote for such fantasy-based policies. He earned high marks from conservative organizations and a perfect 100% from the Christian Coalition. But the League of Conservation Voters never ranked his voting record higher than five (out of 100).

Sen. Craig never hit on me personally, though his anti-gay votes have certainly landed on my back. But every citizen of the Northwest – and the country – has been hit hard by Republican attempts to make reality go away. When denial is elevated to an ideology and allowed to govern, we're all . . . well . . . (sorry!) – screwed.

I'll bet there is some other form of conservatism that isn't mired in pretence and hypocrisy. One with a sense of the past, perhaps, and of caution, forthrightness, courage. Surely the nation could have used it over these last few, interminable, bloody, bankrupting years.

# O Felix Obama: Politics as Storytelling

MAY 2008

Depressed and upset yet again after a day of primary voting that didn't go the way I wanted, I determined to put
myself on a media fast next election day. No radio, no TV!
No inane analysis! No bloggy imbroglio! Just me in my life,
living first-hand the way I should. At least until evening, say,
eight o'clock, when I could absorb the result all at once and
– perhaps – stop thinking about it.

Tuesday arrived. Driving in the silent car, or lounging
blogless in my study, I considered my oft-distracted life.
And most particularly I wondered: Why do I get so deeply
unsettled when these political stories go veering off into the
wrong results?

I do know better. Anyone who lets his personal wellbe-
ing depend on strangers doing politics is surely a fool. The
nations rage, folly marches on, mobs and mountebanks find
each other and their misrule is as common as mud. This
surely is the human condition, and it's our job – each of us –
to fashion a rich and productive life in its muddy midst. Not

to join the mob, and not to get stuck in complaining and handwringing either. Nope. Just realism and a sunny drive to create, love, and enjoy.

Nonetheless. There I was, dank and dispirited at 8:01 after the Pennsylvania primary. It reminded me of a more widespread trauma – that awful Wednesday in November 2004 when so many of us entered a shared and prolonged depression. The 48.3% who voted against the incumbent President simply did not want to believe that militant fundamentalism was what the majority of our country amounted to after all. We had hoped for the High Comedy of restored order. But we ended up with tragic farce: the stupidity of humankind, marching towards catastrophe, banners a-flying and hymns a-singing. If your story reveals your identity, this was a most unwelcome revelation.

Of course, to the winners the day brought a happy ending: Brave leader confronts evil – grateful nation backs him up! America the Godly, fighting against killer pagans. Simple and satisfying, like a cartoon or a martial-arts movie.

❊ ❊ ❊

When I examine these yearnings and their disappointments, I am convinced that what's at work is a profound inner demand for a good story: not just what politics is, but what it means. You could say that politics, in a democracy, is communal storytelling. A story committee numbering millions gets to define which character was (after all) the Hero, what his or her struggles meant, and how the battle came right in the end.

For politics isn't just "theater," as is often observed.

Politics is *narrative*. Storytelling is a primal way to make sense of the world – and applied to politics, it's a way of connecting our private imaginative lives with the public realm (as Hannah Arendt observed). Facts and interpretations are shifty, so when we argue about who we are and what to do next in our national life, we tend to resolve them all into a story-line, a satisfying pattern with good guy, bad guy, sequence of confronting episodes, and resolving outcome. Figuring out the plot of the election is a perennial indoor sport. And when a good ending is obtained, we rejoice, for the election has seemed to validate the world as a good and sensible place, where the Hero wins and the truth comes out.

But when the good ending is denied – when we're on the losing end of an election – we often feel emotions that seem out of proportion. "Hey, it's just politics," I tell myself. But who am I kidding. Something about this communal story roots deep, deep, right into our sense of safety and satisfaction in the world. If the world tells us crappy tales, it's a crappy world. Not where we really wanted to live. If America wants to lie and torture, it's not the America I thought I was living in. I feel weird and misplaced, like I've been written into the wrong tale.

As a young man, I read wise old scholar Frank Kermode's book about story-endings that bring concord out of the discords of life. I've been thinking about it ever since. The stories we remember longest (hundreds or even thousands of years!) shock us convincingly with a potent, final re-ordering of events that changes their meaning – the *peripateia* or reversal of fortune that arises from the Greek hero's secret flaws; the strange glow that emanates from *The Tempest* when its sorcerer-protagonist decides to forego revenge. Rich and strange, these changes. It's not surprising we should desire them for our real-life stories too.

* * *

We believe so much in the power of story that whole religions are organized around it. What's called "the gospel" means of course "good news," *evangel*. What Christians offer is *a news story* so potent that hearing it will transform your very soul. Now that's a good story!

Jesus' story, as it has come to be told, satisfies classic story form that plays on hidden ironies: It goes down when it seems to be going up, then comes up just when it seems dead and done with. While his followers are enjoying the big crowds of Jerusalemites running out to hear the Sermon on the Mount or triumphally parading him into the capital city – Jesus knows this is too good to last. And sure enough, his descent is swift and shocking. Death and burial follow.

But here's the convincing, satisfying twist: Jesus' defeat is his victory. This final reversal isn't just clever, as in an O. Henry tale. Nor is it a disconnected surprise cranked down from the rafters. This story's ending satisfies because it is already built in to the tale's materials – it's a transformation, not just a cute twist. The depressing string of defeats at the hands of imperious conquerors – Jesus' capture, trial, and execution – is *turned into the means* for victory on an unprecedented level: resurrection, redemption, transfiguration. It is a victory that redefines the very meaning of defeat.

That transformation is the key. It exposes the power of

a story with a really good turn. The kind of story that, religious or not, raises the hairs on the back of your neck. *Ah,* says your story-loving mind, *so that's how this strange old world works: defeats hidden in victories, and renewal overcoming even death . . .*

Medieval theologians called this self-reversing plot-line "the Fortunate Fall." Through this lens, our Garden-of-Eden descent into original sin is not seen as tragic or mistaken or even regrettable – No! It was *fortunate*, and it was necessary. *O felix culpa*, O happy sin! Because through it, humanity is transformed from the innocent children of the Garden into death-tested adults, co-inheritors of the universe, even brothers and sisters of the God-Son. Wow. What a story. Paradox, mystery, twistedness. Enigmas locked inside darkness, good news coming out of bad, springtimes out of winters. That's the hair-raising part: This world is deeper than we knew. Maybe better.

Of course all the religions offer powerful stories. The death-and-renewal tale has age-old versions told all around the world. I have come to love parts of Rama's life, from the Indian scripture *Ramayana*. Arjuna's story (the frame-tale of the *Bhagavad Gita*) has done me some good. Occasionally I get encouragement from Navajo stories (love that Turquoise Boy!) and even a couple of Chinook tales from the Columbia River. I admit the stories of Krishna don't move me much, and Mohammed's story is alien to me – I don't know either well enough. But they all apparently pack a spiritual wallop, if you're an attentive hearer.

Story not only tells us who we are. Story changes who we are – it is transformative. Redemptive. Strong magic in it.

\* \* \*

It makes me think that one thing our political stories need is longer time-lines. I wish I could hear more American narratives about people who fought and failed, but stuck to their beliefs, persevered, and in the end brought their principles through to the light. If we hadn't killed them off, Martin Luther King, Jr. or Bobby Kennedy might have embodied such a tale. But we must look elsewhere. Nelson Mandela travelled from twenty-seven years of disappearance and failure in the prison of Robben Island – to a political triumph not just of taking power but of transforming blood into peace. And winning changed him even less than losing. A story like that might remind our politicians that one day's political fight is part of a longer narrative. It might remind them not to sell out so quickly, when met with either adversity or success. It might help them believe that there's a bigger prize than mere advantage. That deeper twists are possible, profounder stories.

For at least part of the political year in which I am writing, Barack Obama has seemed unstoppable. I think it's because, through his story, we get to write a redemptive ending to the miserable experience of the Bush years. It would be a classic reversal: We went through terrible darkness, but it led to an unprecedented moment of national reconciliation. And Obama's story packs a double wallop because it also finishes the "civil rights struggle" story-line, which we love (now that it's part of our past – at least in the national imagination). To put this dramatic finisher to it – a Black man in the Presidency who leads us to higher ground – well, that would be pure pleasure.

Voters seem ready for it. If our story tells us who we are, this redeeming and renewing story would be good news indeed. At least on Inauguration Day. (After that, who knows? Real life stubbornly refuses to stop at the happy ending. And if we have chosen the dazzling newcomer, rather than his long-experienced rivals – that's a definite risk. Will this hero be stubborn enough to persevere through the darkness that, inevitably, must be coming? His *story* says he will. We'll see if he can keep telling it that way.)

# How To Be a Progressive
# (Without Believing in Progress)

Early April, another walk on Powell Butte. Portland's sky-scrapers gleam a few miles off, but here, muffled footfalls thread between pillars of old-growth fir and shaggy cedar, moss-heavy in deep shade, smelling of wet earth and lichen and mushrooms. Then, in a sunny patch, a spate of bright birdsong recalls music I listened to this week. It's a strange feeling, a weird and unobvious connection – must be the echoing forest, I decide, and the free-flowing melisma so joyous and wild.

When I return home I listen some more. It is music from the eleventh century, choral, celestial. I am transported. Words lofted into cathedral spaces praise gentleness, delicacy, lovingkindness. Hildegard of Bingen wrote them. I know of course that her time was bloody full of oppression and swaggering warriors. Yet this music brings suddenly to mind its own echo – that roomful of sculpted medieval Marys I saw at the Met in New York. Sometimes Mary rests the babe on her hip, gazing into his eyes. Sometimes he reaches up a fat little arm. Her face is placid, forgiving, somehow cosmically human. These are stone motets to kindness and mercy, eloquent across the ages – and exactly what Hildegard's music evokes. Both sculpture and music are flowers of a sustained, centuries-long cultural exploration of gentleness – generation after generation a deep cultivation of tenderness and simplicity. I don't know how they did it.

Where, exactly, can a soul go today for training in kindness, yielding? Our bellicose religious movements, our surly politics, our worldslaughtering sciences, our fractured arts: Their worth is great, yet they have forgotten much that was known – and known deeply – a thousand years ago. We are to a large extent beginners when we seek this path.

It makes you wonder about what we call "progress." I've come to see that while some things are better, others are remarkably worse. It just depends on what you decide to measure.

Biologist David Ehrenfeld holds that progress is a myth even in the sciences – where unfashionable knowledge is abandoned, he says, as the leading edge moves forward. The nineteenth century's meticulous attention to morphology and taxonomy, for instance, has faded from living practice – no more Cuviers and Agassizes conveying mastery to successors – while more profitable problems of microbiology and genetics are picked up instead.

We're wowed by the new, even as we forget what we've left behind. It makes us think we're progressing.

As for us – We have better healthcare, but we might not be healthier. We're probably fatter and weaker, though certainly less likely to die of flu or childbirth. We live longer. But do we live better? Without resorting to nostalgia, it is possible to wonder. Stereos we have, but can we play a tune?

And if I look at politics of the last few decades, I see a dogs-breakfast of improvement and reversion. While advancing some aspects of social life like minority civil rights, we've drifted backward toward oligarchic rule that resembles the days of the Robber Barons, enabled by yellow journalism and reactionary priestcraft. We have even allowed core liberties, from the Bill of Rights to *habeas corpus*, to be conned away from us without a fight. It's obvious that we can go backwards in a hurry.

But how can I be a Progressive if I don't believe in Progress?

* * *

Maybe what we liberals ought to stand for is *renewal.* Renewal equally Christian and pagan: Easter cantatas, birds mad with spring, sunshine, ancient trees saved from progress, cities rebuilt after neglect and despair. Renewal would be recognition of error that we've grown invested in. It would be truthtelling. Discarding of dead husks. Repentance. Starting again from wherever we find ourselves.

I think liberals have been as invested in the fantasy of progress as the hairiest Social-Darwinian tycoon. To turn liberals into this other kind of progressive, we might try dropping programs or values that aren't working – even if they were once shibboleths of the righteous left. Neverending welfare checks? Abortion anytime, anywhere? Environmentalism based on Eden fantasies? When the words have hardened into slogans, liberals should try listening to the music. There we may hear answers that better honor our life together.

Renewal would mean welcoming new allies. I have in mind a kind of *productive populism*, committed to the dignity of work: an alliance of moms, truck-drivers, office-workers, unionists, small business entrepreneurs and farmers. They'd know better than to organize an economy around parasitic global corporations and inherited wealth. They'd value actual work, not work-shirking legalisms. And not speculation.

Renewal brings us back to ourselves. It tells the truth, faces facts, accepts adjustment. It is strangely both circular and linear – curving back to that starting point, yet turning it into the *starting-anew* point.

The motet returns to its beginning, flightlike, fuguelike, new and old again, a song just like life. Hildegard knew this. Those anonymous sculptors knew it. Moms everywhere probably know it. For progressives who are listening, maybe an earthy renewal – not the fantasy of progress – is our real calling.

# City Gods and Sacred Waters: A Dispersed Essay

SUMMER 2006

I'm staring into a 1.4 billion dollar hole in the ground. It's a twenty-minute stroll from my neighborhood, located near cultural institutions (opera and museum), and by far the largest public-works project in this city's history. And it's a sewer.

Well, a sewer upgrade. Portland calls it the Big Pipe. At present, Portland's nineteenth-century sewers combine household waste with street runoff. It goes to treatment plants of course, but more than a modicum of rain (1/8 inch in an hour) overwhelms the system and dumps the overflow straight into the Willamette River. In 1991, under orders from the EPA, the city began a 20-year project to install fourteen miles of jumbo pipe on both sides of the river to collect the overflow, hoist it over some riverside bluffs, and transport it all miles away to a treatment plant near the Columbia River. A mighty endeavor! By the end of this year, 1991's six billion gallons of spillage will be cut by two thirds. By 2011, our fifty annual overflow events should diminish to a negligible three or four per year.

So I'm looking at a twenty-two-foot turd-flume. And, oddly, thinking about God.

❊ ❊ ❊

This sanctified spin comes to me from Joel Kotkin's recent book *The City*, which declares that cities must be "safe, busy, and sacred." Kotkin observes that urban civilizations, Egyptian or Mesopotamian, first developed more or less because of the need to control scarce or seasonal water. Priests kept calendars, engineers learned to draw straight and plan big, kings appointed bureaucracies. And at the city-center of all this controlling: a really big temple or ziggurat, where priests made sure the gods kept the water cycle going.

Those were sacred cities all right, epic in scale, dwarfing the miserable subjects who slaved for them. But it is hard to make the application to a twenty-first century city. Where would our sacredness be? *What* would it be? And would water be connected to that sacredness now, as then?

I don't know yet. But well into my second decade here as a Portland transplant from desert Los Angeles, I still feel a tingle of blessing every time I take one of our many river-bridges, no matter my mood or graceless state. There's a link somehow to sacredness, and I want to explore it.

That's what walking would be for.

❊ ❊ ❊

On Sundays around eleven, when local restaurants spill loiterers onto the sidewalks, it's for lazy-brunch not for after-church. I sidle past. This is in the Hawthorne District where I live, one of Portland's many understated-yet-hip neighborhoods, walkably close to downtown. Oregon's population is the least-churched in the United States, except for Nevada. Most people hereabouts just garden on Sundays. Or go kayaking. Or take a walk, as I am doing today (when I should be grading papers). Whatever "sacred" means in Portland, it's not located in steeplehouses or cathedrals.

It could be somewhere near our river, though. Because cleaning up the Willamette is a commitment that has spanned generations and produced moments of cooperation and vision that, frankly, you'd think beyond our reach. We're not a rich state and we're no wiser than anyone else. Yet Oregon citizens established the nation's first environmental government agency, in 1938, by passing a (then-novel) ballot initiative creating the Oregon State Sanitary Authority specifically for the purpose. Its successor, the Department of Environmental Quality (DEQ), is now overseeing the grand project of the Big Pipe.

And Portlanders are paying for it all alone: no federal or state dollars. Our sewer rates, already nearly the highest in the nation, are projected to jump another 35% (at least) before it's all through. But you won't hear any complaining. None.

\* \* \*

So I'm crossing the Willamette River that divides Portland to see a simple thing: a kind of gutter. It has received a national award, this gutter, from the American Society of Landscape Architects. Along a downtown sidestreet, four planter-boxes of concrete are inset between street and sidewalk. Breaks in the curb let gutter-water run in and settle amongst the newly-planted sedges, shrubs, and trees. A Modigliani of crossing bricks and curbs contrasts pleasingly with cast-iron grates slotted in a repeating wave pattern.

Things grow, water perks down through the cleansing soil instead of adding to the burden of flushwater and stormwater. It's a small good thing: one place where things are going right. Model, mitzva, yoga of living. Nothing epic, just a small lyric of good design and intentionality.

But I see gestures like this everywhere as I return over the Hawthorne Bridge and walk back through the neighborhood: bioswales to collect runoff at St. Philip Neri Catholic Church *and* the New Seasons across the street from it, and another at the middle school just around the corner. I see green roofs. Home downspouts disconnected and played into gardens. Little songs, local hums.

* * *

A rainy day: splashes on my window, beading up or trickling. I stand rooted, surprised, my eye seeing them suddenly as letters, *characters* really – a trick I have surely never experienced before.

I had been practicing my Chinese calligraphy, holding the brush just so, making the downstroke, the crossing, the finish. And there they are on the window, characters forming and dissolving in clear water. My mind flips wildly between modes of language and picture. Was that *strength*? *Tree*?

It doesn't stop there. Walking by newsstands I misread headlines habitually, finding poems and silly jokes. Political *panties*? Airplanes with *shy marshals*? And while passing conversations of strangers, my ever-weaker hearing makes odd catches, phrases overheard, underheard. In this shifting world people say surreal and elevated things, I am a student of their philosophy, and the news on someone's radio announces a word-salad of apocalypse and buffoonery.

What was that?

❖ ❖ ❖

Kotkin's view of cities as "safe, busy, and sacred" echoes that famous formulation from a generation ago, when mountain poet Gary Snyder defined an ethic of "good, wild, and sacred." At that time most of us assumed *wild* must be the opposite of *city*.

But I've come to see that wildness isn't a place, it's a process. When synapses snap together in a new thought, that's wild. Wildness is in us, as it is in everything alive. When elements in a system – even an urban system – creatively mesh and produce surprising results, dire or wonderful, that's wild. "City making is among the most complex and difficult human undertakings – as complex as life itself," one of our best city-scholars reminds us (Douglas Kelbaugh) – so it's not going to jump to life off a planner's proposal. It may evolve, though, if you let it. A city is an ecosystem of desires and solutions, aggressions and cooperations. A city can shock, nourish, kill. It's a kind of wild place.

But is it "good"? Americans expect virtue down on the farm and vice in the big, bad city. Yet where do most art and music and ideas come from, if not from urban civilization? Indeed, even our Bible, though it starts in a garden, ends in a City of God. We are taught by this to imagine a trajectory toward an ever more complex and rewarding interconnection with each other. Exquisite possibility: the blab of the pave, the breakdown dance and shuffle (says Whitman, wild poet of New York City).

Cities: good and wild. That, of course, leaves sacred.

* * *

A place like the Keller Fountain might convince anyone. It's another week, another walk, and I have been sitting here for a half hour before I know it, observing, connecting, retreating. There's a comfortable plaza, recessed below sidewalk-level in front of the Keller's plunging waterfalls. And, with a few midmorning others, I sit unconsciously held within the drama of all that watersound, the mist that plays games in my nose and lungs coming and going with downtown smells and early-summer heat and carswoosh. The Keller's massed revetments of squared-off concrete form wading pools that spill broad shining twenty-foot falls, while nubbly concrete plates underfoot come strangely alive in channels of water slotted through them and gurgling beneath them like it was a solidified mountain meadow. Somehow these Cascade pleasures have been wedged into a tiny sloping city block across from Portland's civic auditorium right in the midst of busy one-way streets.

It's a bit of urban magic – a place of open privacy, as only the best cityscapes are. Lord knows I've depended on wild places for spiritual solace, for climbs and solitudes all across the Sierras and Cascades. But you cannot be alone, together, in public like this, except where there *is* a public: that is, in a city. It's a deep pleasure.

A couple of disreputable city characters have sprawled on the grass at the upper end. I'd call them bums but we don't talk that way anymore. They and their shopping carts don't match the picturesque conifers that lean like Japanese stone-pines though most of them turn out to be plain old northwest lodgepole. A teenager talks on her cell phone just across from where I've been sitting on the wide warm steps. How she chatters. Nature grows the trees and pulls the water over the brink. People come and sit and leave. Sun shines off the condo tower.

\* \* \*

Keller Fountain was the far end of my day's foot journey, so now I return through the thick of downtown. Just normal city walking, I guess. The loitering toughs I saw meeting customers on street corners last year have been removed. Now it's mostly just well-dressed businesspeople, kids with droopy pants, tourists; questionable types are really a rarity in our squeaky-clean town. I wonder if my bourgeois standards aren't a little narrow.

My idea was to visit famous city fountains, but instead I'm noticing how the non-famous mixes with the fancy, as I peoplewatch and do some loitering myself. Here's a sidewalk-mounted fountain that will never make the guidebook, ordinary bricks painted motel-room-beige and built five-square into pools with runways between them. No placard. Some peeling. Might be mid-sixties. Elsewhere along the way, real art and whatnot: a brushed-steel Lee Kelly sculpture; a bronze pioneer family clutching Bible and ragdoll and staring into their noble future. Every block its excess and its surprise. I detour a few blocks to enjoy the tasteless, expensive pleasures of Lawrence Gallery, where bronze boy-nudes do backwards swan dives, girl-nudes rotate on pedestals, and child-nudes disturb the boundary between pederasty and kitsch. Honestly, you've gotta see this. Little shops, weenie carts, winos. What's that art-word I learned for random this-n-that combinations . . . *bricolage.* A nice sound. Bricolage of people, things, tastes. City.

And here are two of those famous Lovejoy Columns, old viaduct supports scrolled and sketched almost sixty years ago by the still-palpable hand of railroad worker Tom Stefopoulos, now preserved in this courtyard to help us honor and remember and take stock. A charcoaled ibex leaps over a fervent slogan. Zebra stripes surround an edge just for the joy of it. We need more of this. A city must have its past woven visibly, tangibly into its present or it's not much more than an impacted suburb. Must weave, too, the forgotten and the famous and the best-left-unmentioned. City.

✸ ✸ ✸

The Pearl District, where I've left my car, has been transformed in one short decade from industrial warehouses, art galleries, and cheap lofts into endless half-million-and-up townhouses. The Pearl is, uh, *nice.* Woven of money and amnesia.

Which could describe the Pearl's newest famous park, Tanner Springs, my last stop today. I have read that it recycles rainwater, cleansing it through "biotopes" of sandy regimented plantings and a tranquil pool. But to do so it has had to banish children and dogs and picnics. What's left feels arid and one-dimensional. I sit on a bench halfway along the diagrammatically zigzag path and don't feel any buzz at all – there's nothing going on here except what's been planned.

But swooping out of Tanner's downslope pool is an undulating palisade of recycled railroad rails, leaning crazily, inset with bits of blue glass. It draws me, and soon I discover that up at street level a wooden boardwalk has been sinuously cut to match. Aggressively artificial yet strangely inviting, it's full of a rowdy imagination and wildness.

Too bad the park isn't.

* * *

My calligraphic practicing continues. Here's my best one. *Shui*: water.

See how it flows. Or might, if done well.

* * *

Warm weather returns to our unreliable early summer, and a couple miles from my house three people sit at picnic tables under aspens. An acre of blacktop bakes around them and edges up to the single-story schoolrooms of Jim Bridger Elementary. But breaking the desolation is the aspen-oasis, and when Kelley Webb waves me over I'm glad to join them. Kelley has quit her job with regional Metro government to do things like recycle buildings (for a profit) and remodel schoolyards (for love). She's in a meeting with Patricia and Dave, fellow members of Urban Water Works.

The big plan for Urban Water Works and its school-parent collaborators – Jennifer and Nancy are two moms weeding in the sunshine a few yards away – is to redirect roof-water and runoff into this parklet they've created over the last year. I count seven downspouts on the wide U of classrooms around us and try to imagine a year's worth of Oregon rainfall. Instead of barreling straight into overtaxed sewers, runoff *from* here will *stay* here, running through a watercourse into a pond to support shade trees, spireas and carexes and cattails, grasses and foam-flowers and whatever else might move in. Nature-gentrification. Soon the neighborhood will soon be hopping – and fluttering and splashing – in a whole new way. With child-play and kid-song and wide-eyed wonderment in the mix.

But today Kelley and her cohort are evaluating school-board worries. Kelley tells me: "There's definitely a fear of standing water. Six inches is all we can allow; we'll need an overflow pipe . . ." They hash out solutions while the moms go on weeding.

School bureaucrats are apparently also obsessing over the oasis itself, full of possibly unauthorized plants. "Yeah," says Patricia, "there's a fear of wildness too." Urban Water Works has already modulated plantings so they don't appear too bohemian or out of control. "It has to look intentional," she explains. I nod wisely, as if I know.

But all I know, really, is this: that I recessed on grade-school blacktops in hundred-degree Los Angeles heat and survived it. But that the occasional month in the mountains, playing amongst trees and birdsong and creekwater, left my imagination impregnated with a durable mood of imaginative possibility, a greenworld tucked into my neural net.

And that Nancy and Jennifer have lucky kids.

\* \* \*

I thought I heard music. Or was it just city noises?

I've had Olivier Massiaen on my CD player lately, his *musique concrète* that plays with everyday sounds. And brooding compositions by Victoria Jordanova, banging strums and silences and mysterious sonic gestures. Now – unexpectedly – my ear is reading the world's random sound as music too – possible music, maybe-music. What was that?

It is the *feng* and the *shui* isn't it – music: wind and water: flow. Breathe in, breathe out. Nothing controlled; nothing saved for later. It's all water. As are we.

Sound washes over us and vanishes. What was that?

\* \* \*

Once America was all about Mesopotamian-scale projections of power over nature: Manhattan Project, Bonneville, Grand Coulee, Hoover – controlling, channeling, damming, diverting. Mastery.

But isn't it remarkable how many of our investments nowadays aim toward *lessening* control, even reversing it? – so that the lifegiving complexity of nature can be allowed to solve the problems our pseudo-mastery has created – flood, pollution, dying ecosystems? It's a countermelody of undoing. Sometimes it too is gigantic, fugal. The Willamette

River is a Superfund site – that's as big as it gets, un-doing on a grand scale. As is our Big Pipe. But part of the Big Pipe is a program to encourage individual Portlanders to disconnect those downspouts, and people are doing it all around town. There was no personal buy-in to atom-splitting or dam-building. This is different in mood and meaning, different in spirit. This is not mastery but relinquishment.

What Portland does with its water *is* its spirituality. And it is the opposite of the hierarchic, epic spirituality of the old temples and kings, thunderous God-houses and domineering priests. This is dispersed, democratized: a lyric each of us can sing quietly. An eco-roof. A creek. A downspout. It is scalable in ways the old mastery never was, connecting from city to school right down to the most private moment – high or low! – the hand reaching for the flush-handle, the drop of water on the window.

And isn't that what a spiritual life is? A perception of connectedness – to God, to others, to the living world – a connectedness that may not be obvious, may be subterranean or downright invisible – but that's real nonetheless? It may be that the sacred is, simply, connection to *wildness* that we cannot control or predict. Wherever wildness breaks out is grace and a glimpse of the spirit – whether in tangled bank or cityscape – ecosystem or mind, art or music, solitary ramble or solidarity of the plaza.

I see this yielding spirit in Portland since that's where my boots are always on the ground. But I hear similar news from all over. It's *repentance*: undoing our errors, revisiting our sins, making amends. Salmon being invited back to the Elwha (Washington) and the St. Georges (Maine) and even the Thames and the Loire: dams big and small coming out by the hundreds. No doubt that old habit of control can never completely leave us. Maybe just *having* the counter-thought is a fair start; that we remember the other accountancies of yielding, praying, co-existing – and make room for them.

Far off there are melting icecaps, events almost too huge and strange to contemplate. Our grandchildren will have to face them, though, and find for themselves the faith and the means to go on. Maybe the best we can do is impregnate the present with as much green hope as possible.

❖ ❖ ❖

September has come. My walks are almost over. On the day Portland announces (big fanfare) that it has hooked up the Westside Big Pipe, a heavy rain mocks the celebration by forcing . . . just what it is supposed to prevent: yet another sewer discharge into the river.

An occasion for irony, then. And what could be the spiritual meaning of that?

Plenty. The message of water is that you don't control it – you ride it, and it rides you. Let it mock us! This is a better god, I think, than the one of embroidered robes and ceremonies. Let us be undercut, let the water flow, let us be carried. Let us look low as well as high for this divinity. Perhaps he – or she – is also a drinking god, bibulous and joking and pissing. Look, here's a tavern – this is Portland after all – let us step in and drink to our higher and lower selves, to outbreaks of sacred wildness in country and city and all that dwell therein. To an urbane spirituality unafraid of sewers and winos and good intentions, willing to fight for them with every artful dodge, every doing – and every undoing – we can think of.

# I Am Already Dead

He looked at me with a strange calm intensity. "It does not matter. I am already dead," said Raed, my Palestinian student.

Though it is more than twenty years ago, the moment is still vivid. His short-sleeved plaid shirt, not fashionable but neat and orderly like everything about Raed. His slim body, slight shoulders, long face. He was dark-haired as you'd expect, his skin a light olive, but it is the eyes that remain the center of this eidetic image: large, dark-irised, and unblinking, as if they were never going to flinch, not ever. That's it, I suppose. They were *older* than they should have been, their earnestness a burden not a redemption.

It was not a threatening moment, I hope this is clear. Raed was disciplined and respectful, his work thorough. He must have been in his early twenties like most of the Jordanian and Egyptian and various diaspora'd Palestinian students our second-rate college paid its bills with. Back home somewhere were either militaries sending them for engineering degrees, or daddies with oil money or government sinecures. But Raed was the rare one untouched by cynicism or swagger. He stood in my faculty office as late-afternoon light poured through the Venetian blinds, and after we had gone over his essay – after I had tried to be the good teacher, the humanist, the cultivator of souls – Raed had ventured this one moment, direct and undisguised. "I am already dead," he said, gazing straight at me.

He meant of course that he was completely in the hands of the divinity and hence there was no difference – dead here was alive in the heavens with the faithful. He meant of course that he accepted whatever hard fate or violent duty might come to him. He meant of course *intifada.*

But what *that* meant was something full of the pure spirituality of youth, that yearning for clarity. "It does not matter what happens to me. I do not worry. I am already dead." Probably he would never read Kierkegaard, but he gave perfect allegiance to that dangerous absolutism: *Purity of heart is to will one thing.* Yet what human life is about one thing only? I ask this in all earnestness – aren't our lives about many things, duties and necessities and, yes, pleasures that never, ever come out neat and even? What mature human spirit has not set aside black and white certainties for the truer agonies, and delights, of a walk of faith (not certitude)? I have little doubt that Raed's body is long since machine-gunned or self-exploded, its flesh expended before it ever tasted the merely human fulfillments of our difficult world. The mixed and impure stuff of real human life.

I don't doubt that Raed found death before he found life, a paradox but not a spiritual one.

\* \* \*

I wonder what it is that transforms a religion into a force against life.

This is not a swipe at Islam. It is a genuine question. As far as I can tell, every religion takes this strange dark turn sometimes. If not usually. How does the miraculous-creator-life-force God become the grim anti-God of death and negation?

Once a brother and I were disputing about something political – it might have been the carnage of American war-making, probably Vietnam. Inevitably our quarrel took a religious turn. "*Goodness,*" he sneered – "what's that? The Bible says 'All our righteousness is as filthy rags.' Look at the Old Testament. God kills the wicked, period. God doesn't worry about niceness, does He?"

This was a long time ago, so perhaps this believer's view has matured. We don't talk now, so I wouldn't know. But I do know this attitude of contempt for merely human virtue is commonplace in the pulpits and pews of our home-grown fundamentalism. Kindness, meekness, tolerance, peace? Why bother. On the radio, one cross-country drive, a preacher with a heavy southern accent – J. Vernon McGee, I believe – spit out the selfsame sneer to his listeners. "Ah don't b'LIEVE in a God that's all NICEY-nice! God HATES sin and He will NOT tolerate it!" The "nicey-nice" part is an exact quote, indelible. Disturbing, isn't it?

The point was that our normal scale of values had no relevance. The human versions of love and goodness were too befouled to consider. *Doctrine* told us what these words meant, not experience. "God's standards are not ours," they would say.

So what is "love"? What does this word mean, this word so infused with humanity, with the tenderness of motherhood, the fire of loving touch, the nobility of self-sacrifice, the everydayness of getting along? These things are the *substance* which the word merely references. What's left when these are removed?

What's left is mere idea. Abstraction. The official line is that "love" really means saving sinners from hellfire. Since this is the greatest good imaginable, anything else is irrelevant, perhaps a dangerous distraction. Thus "love" is a doctrine, a thin pure idea far above mere feelings, mere consequences, mere pain. Not an action where flesh and spirit imperfectly, tenderly intertwine.

It is an example of letting the words go empty.

\* \* \*

As a youthful Christian I was more *thorough* than most of the folks sampling our dilute suburban evangelicalism. Fundamentalist words were certainly spoken – the realness of hell, the absolute literalness of the Bible, wives submitting to husbands, the whole thing. But in fact these middle-class Baptists were a relaxed bunch, not much concerned with punishing or demanding. Probably they were very loving to one another. But I wanted something fierce and strong. I don't know why, exactly. Perhaps I had too much to prove.

Youthful idealism easily hardens into this kind of abstract idolatry. The black-and-white demands of earnest youngsters ought to be something older folks help them grow out of. Gently. But even the kindliest of elders, when saddled with such a brutal official language, have no way to do so.

I remember hearing nothing moderating from my fellow congregants. If I expressed some all-or-nothing fervor, some life-consuming zeal, they were honor-bound to applaud it. (I wonder how much guilt they must have felt at their own mixed lives and choices?) Driven by my own guilt, I constructed ever more demanding scaffolds on which to execute my sinful flesh. Naturally, I couldn't live there for long. And as I slid toward desperation, a mysterious grace prevented me from spiraling into self-destruction, as so many secretly gay kids do. But this grace, this moderating humanity, came from outside – not inside – my sad little religion.

* * *

This human story we live is sobering, isn't it. So much of what befalls us comes self-created of temperament, leaning, the quirks of mind that drive us to pour good energy after bad in self-defeating heroics – or that might allow us to make our circumstances better. Lighten up, redirect that passion? Never occurred to me.

Armand was as dark as Raed, but it was his parents who had been born over there. And he was a bit younger too – a high-schooler early-admitted into my research paper course. When his turn in the Prof's office came up, he leaned forward in his chair, brimming with physicality, earnestness. "I don't know if this is what I'll end up working on in my medical career, but . . ." He was shy about claiming any virtue. He wanted to do his course-long research topic on children's AIDS in the third world, he said.

And his work as it emerged was direct, concrete, focused on real children and imperfect ameliorations. So good I copied off sections to use for handouts, examples of how to think and dig and present. I helped him a little in this but – teachers will know what I mean – he would have done excellent work no matter what. He looked straight into the realities, to see what they were and how to act against them, with them. As I worked with Armand I came to feel something almost a little military about this – a standing in the breach. He was brave and resolute, but these qualities had somehow been translated into kindness-in-action, not bellicose purity. It was charming to see, of course, but it was more than that. It made me notice how I had stopped thinking much about these huge intractable problems far away. The suffering of others. It's what an older person can learn from a younger, sometimes.

Somewhere in the eucalyptus haze of Berkeley, Armand works toward his destiny. Studying. Growing up I suppose. Or in his case, growing into an already sturdy structure of belief and action. Already when I knew him he was past the slogans and the absolutes. Unlike poor Raed, *already dead* at twenty-two, Armand had found a rarer gift.

At seventeen, he was already alive.

# Under Pressure We Make Lists

AUGUST 2008

For the length of this whole book I have been fighting the tendency. Every time I write about these years of political catastrophe I feel myself falling into a kind of vortex, mesmerized and outraged and soon listing the abuses, counting the reasons, tallying the details, the laws, the clear violations, the lack of response, the names, the wounds, the deaths. Unable to stop. Delete. Delete. Start over. And again the list spools out onto the page and takes over.

But I notice that I'm not the only one. Over and over I see other writers, accomplished and well-known, drawn off the road into the endless ruts of "and, and, and," listing obsessively what we all know too well already. It's clear they can't help themselves either, the buildup of sheer plain obvious self-evident-evidence maddens them, galls them, drives their shapely sentences off the road, wrecks their elegantly modulated paragraphs until once again we hear the ranting, shouting frustration that is the keynote of our time.

Why? Partly because of that very self-evidentness. This is the time of official shamelessness: torture and lying as policy, discussed – *literally* – in the Oval Office, by blank-faced pols. For seven years that have felt like seven decades – a moral lifetime, at least – we, the Americans, have been their impotent dupes. What could we feel but outrage? And the list is the literary form of outrage: sputtering, overflowing, angry, obsessive. In it we are reduced to raining blows on the target because nothing else works – not truth, not decency, not tradition, not law. So we continue to hammer on this brick wall, even if it's with our heads.

Why? Why would you hammer it with your head?

Because
it
is
a
brick
wall
!

❊ ❊ ❊

A pause for perspective. I notice that most of the *Declaration of Independence* is a list. You can probably visualize it: The lower two-thirds of the handsome broadside enumerates some twenty-seven grievances supporting the case for separation from Great Britain, in language at once restrained and seething (nice trick). In this intensity you can feel the long decades of mounting frustration that spawned clandestine actions, manifestos, pamphlets, destruction of merchandise, domestic terror, and finally armed resistance and war.

*Twenty-seven.* I wonder if we're up to that yet. (Who am I kidding, I have hit that in a single sentence, more than once.)

Of course the lists we write and rewrite really do resemble that list in the Declaration: a roster of abuses and usurpations. Such as the seven listed on the Amherst, Massachusetts Town Warrant for impeachment (November 2006). The four of the Arcata, California Resolution (February 2006). The four of the Carrboro, North Carolina Resolution (March 2006). The impeachment resolutions of eighty-nine other cities and counties. And the thirty-five articles of impeachment finally offered in Congress against the President by Rep. Dennis Kucinich in May of 2007.

Ineffectual. Useless. Yet somehow better – far better – than the alternative: mute acquiescence.

And as I say, under pressure even the best of us resorts to the list. William Faulkner, on the surely daunting occasion of his Nobel Address, retreated to almost artless listing. What do mere writers have to offer, he asked, under the cloud of atomic annihilation? Only "love and honor and pity and pride and compassion and sacrifice . . ." And, in the next paragraph of this famously brief address, he both *repeats* and *lengthens* the same list. And then adds a third list close by! Why? "Our tragedy today is a general and universal physical fear so long sustained by now that we can even bear it." Such pain, such fear – only the list can give it voice. And and and.

So to the ghost of Molly Ivins; to Bob Herbert, David James Duncan, and a hundred other writers whom I admire and emulate; to all of us who have tried to write our way to some kind of cleansing clarity and ended up instead in the rankling murk of lists: We are in good company.

\* \* \*

With hardly any logical shape except "and," the list is the form of excess emotion, of overflow plunging down the course of least resistance. It's practically raw data.

It shows up in poetry as well as politics. Elizabeth Barrett Browning's "How do I love thee? Let me count the ways . . ." resorts to listing because her passions threaten to overwhelm. And the list works just as well for darker emotions. Victorian poet Matthew Arnold, standing at Dover Beach, elegizes a world (his world, rapidly becoming ours) which

> Hath really neither joy, nor love, nor light,
> Nor certitude, nor peace, nor help for pain . . .

His six-noun pile-up is an emotional *q.e.d.*, somehow hard to dispute. Certainly few images have had a more eerily prophetic truth than the clincher that follows:

> And we are here as on a darkling plain
> Swept with confused alarms of struggle and flight,
> Where ignorant armies clash by night.

*And we are here* indeed, surrounded by the ignorant armies of holocaust-deniers, creationists, global-warming doubters . . . and so soon back from poetry to war and politics! Once, as far back as Homer, it was considered grand to catalogue the hero's armor or the names of his opponents. Today, only Whitman's anti-heroic lists ring true, casting the light of divinity onto the particles and pieces of the ordinary world, mullein and pokeweed and your face and mine.

But our collective response to the crisis of the last seven years – so far from heroic – doesn't even rise to this level. Neither heroic nor anti-heroic, our category today is really the pathetic: embodied perhaps in the vacillating, emasculated J. Alfred Prufrock, who asks – *whines* – "Should I, after tea and cakes and ices, / Have the strength to force the moment to its crisis?" Prufrock lists as many reasons for inaction as a congressional Democrat. They shall wear the bottoms of their trousers rolled.

❖ ❖ ❖

Yet across the span of years, it is not the Declaration's anger but its love – its poetry – that moves us. At the top of the famous page is a briefer list. Unlike the furious, exhaustive inventory at the bottom, this little list is so brief, so ripe, so generous of spirit it seems ready to engender invisible multitudes: From *life, liberty, pursuit of happiness,* endowed by a creator-god, might come Love of truth. Love of neighbor. Love of those who will follow . . . No need to list them all, for they are truly a world implicit. A universe in a grain of sand. The opposite of a list: a seed.

As I write this essay, thinking of the end of my book, I walk a lake path in the North Cascades. Around me is abundance, green and flowered and winged. There's a temptation to catalogue what I'm seeing but my heart rebels. Enough of guide books, binoculars and life-lists. Instead, a single miracle flies ahead of me: It's a tanager, flash of crimson borne on yellow wings through the darkling forest. For a time it accompanies me, reappearing and vanishing along the solitary trail. Wrestling with demons, I wonder what kind of answer it is – but in some interior space I already know. Like everything real, it needs no words to collapse the house of lies. Factual, irreducible, beautiful, it need only exist. This is what we rest upon, while the maniacs rage and pretend.

A slow-motion junta has tried to remake the American experiment in freedom into a godly military monarchy (that is, an idolatry), governed from the wings by corporate profiteers. If we fail to name this evil, expose it, and bury it, then generations to follow will surely have to face it in some newly virulent form. But to undertake this duty we will need to stand on more than outrage. We will need to make poetry of our desperation, as the Founders did. We will have to love our moment, declare our values, and act for the generations.

Brief lists, perseverance, and long vistas.

# Epilogue – Night Thoughts and Music, Three Days before Election

## POLITICS AS A HUMANE AND HOPEFUL ART

For years I have considered my obsession with politics as a fool's errand. Every morning the newspapers. Then the blogs. Driving anywhere, the hourly bulletins. Battles, partial truths, my side, your side – surely a waste of spirit in an expense of shame. And since 2004 I have been only more compelled, more horrified. We become a nation of proxy torturers, consumers of propaganda, fans of war. I cannot change it, I cannot relinquish it.

Like most nature writers I am a Thoreauvian, and so I take my walks, consider the clouds, the starlight, spindrift mortality and ever-toppling trees. I try to rise above, as Henry David would insist, by *sinking in.* Sometimes it works, and my creekbed goes all pebbly with stars. But next morning I am back at it, what novelist E.M. Forster called *this life of anger and telegrams.* I can't seem to help myself.

"Politics – so superficial," admonishes the sage of Walden.

Portland becomes rainy, the calendar turns. The elections

of 2008 approach and I am a fool of cold fear and exuberant polling numbers. I have far, far too much invested in next Tuesday. So I seek out music, that higher plane where even waiting seems good for me. In time a slender pianist appears, a master from afar in elegant black dress, and I abandon myself to her impetuous Chopin, all whitewater risks and limpid adagios. Ravel follows, and the twentieth century seems somehow less awful, I can think of a way to smile at passing dissonance. An hour disappears, and the room is transfixed, astonished.

Yet obsession won't let me go. When our pews light up at intermission, I look around and I see politics, politics for certain even in this renovated sanctuary. These hundred-odd strangers – what have we done but entered a commons, a collective self? The Public Realm, where music exists, and all the arts. It would be a lie to pretend it were not politics to maintain what we have dubbed the Old Church, to pay a tax, to select European music, to listen in a roomful of education and privilege.

True enough. Yet there is more here, far more. When strangers share this decorum, when doors open democratically to any who would listen, when this Korean musician commits her life to beauty and its difficult conveyance, and finds a living doing so, and carries it even to this edge of the earth, some kind of magic has appeared. Our collective self is not only a mob, a direct-mail target, an object of self-interest and manipulation. Sometimes we are the instrument of transcendence.

\* \* \*

Despite myself, I am breathless for a new leader, a new start, even though every presidency of my lifetime – I was born in 1950 – has ended as tragedy (excepting those that turned into farce). Eisenhower, leaving us his sad warning of a domestic military-industrial enemy he himself refused to confront. Presidents slain and banished. Texans lying us into wars. Fake cowboys. And the bodice ripper. Remember the Peace Dividend? Gone. All gone. A roster of tragedy, missed opportunity, fakery, squandered capital. So why in the world would I allow myself hope, on the eve of another presidency?

Because if tragedy is our fate, it is a doom found in wrestling with demons, facing terrible challenges, and that is a matter of courage and determination. Let failure come: We are here to fight it out.

Even Orpheus ends tragically – and *his* songs prevailed against the gates of hell! The magic was not the less, just because it all ended badly. The singing was worth it. Watching the demons give way, even if only for a while. Yes, our feet are dirty, our spirits lag, in the end we will not perfect our lives, and we will leave too much behind in salt grief and tears.

But then – we begin again. For some part of this story, things will go well and we will remake the world – singing together, you might say. And then . . . and then. We will have to do it yet again.

Even Thoreau fell victim to hope. He went to jail over an appalling war, a society of corrupting slavery. There in a Concord cell he wrote the very manual of political transcendence, *Civil Disobedience*: ten pages that, a generation later, would inspire Gandhi in a South African jail, and then reach Martin Luther King; words that would transform America, India – and South Africa to boot, Mandela picking up where Gandhi left off and creating his miracle of resistance. Transformation. Magic.

Sometimes we are part of a transcendence. Politics is our collective art. Wait, the lights are down, here comes a new master, elegant, our Representative Man. We will take risks, we will know disappointment. And beauty.

# Notes

## What We Love Will Save Us

**"Loves":** Stephen Dunn, *Landscape at the End of the Century: Poems* (New York: Norton, 1991) 81-94.

## On Pleasure

*lickerous* is an older spelling I prefer – now usually *lickerish* or *liquorish*.

## Six Good Places

**Some 75 percent of the developed world. . . a UN report:** United Nations Population Division, *World Urbanization Prospects: The 1999 Revision.* http://www.un.org/esa/population/publications/wup1999/urbanization.pdf.

**Christopher Alexander:** Christopher Alexander, Sara Ishikawa, Murray Silverstein, *A Pattern Language: Towns, Buildings, Construction* (New York: Oxford, 1977).

**Geographer and historian Jay Appleton:** *The Experience of Landscape* (London: Wiley, 1975).

**Paul Shepard:** See for example his excellent last (and posthumous) book, *Coming Home to the Pleistocene,* ed. Florence R. Shepard (Washington, D.C.: Island, 1998).

## Poetry on the Elliptical

**"It was enough to hollow us out":** Joanna Klink, "Auroras." *Circadian* (New York: Penguin, 2007) 1.

## Forgiving the Present

**"the relatively recent phenomenon"**: Hannah Arendt, "Truth and Politics," in *The Portable Hannah Arendt.* Peter Baehr, ed. (New York: Penguin, 2000), 564.

**"organized lying, dominating the public realm"**: Arendt, "Truth and Politics," in Baehr, ed. 549.

**"rewriting contemporary history"** and **"every known and established fact can be denied"**: Arendt, "Truth and Politics," in Baehr, ed. 564.

**"The ideal subject of totalitarian rule"**: Hannah Arendt, *Origins of Totalitarianism*, "Ideology and Terror" (New York: Harcourt Brace, 1979) 474. Arendt develops this crucial point of in many places – linking it to isolation, the disappearance of public space, the corruption of language, and the divorce from reality that governs totalitarian systems. See especially the third volume, *Totalitarianism.*

**over half the public:** according to the Harris Poll taken just before the presidential election, "62 percent believe[d] that Saddam Hussein had strong links to Al Qaeda." "Iraq, 9/11, Al Qaeda and Weapons of Mass Destruction: What the Public Believes Now." Harris Poll #79, 21 October 2004. http://www.harrisinteractive.com/harris_poll/index.asp?PID=508.

**"common and factual reality itself"**: Arendt, "Truth and Politics," in Baehr, ed. 552.

**"the sense by which we take our bearings in the real world"** and **"[C]onsistent lying"**: Arendt, "Truth and Politics," in Baehr, ed. 568-69.

**"Inspect every piece of pseudoscience"**: Richard Dawkins, *Unweaving the Rainbow* (New York: Houghton Mifflin, 1998) 142.

**"The quality of childhood"**: Dawkins 144.

**"Justice will take us millions of intricate moves"**: William Stafford, "Thinking for Berky," in *The Darkness Around Us Is Deep: Selected Poems.* Robert Bly, ed. (New York: Harper, 1993) 38.

**Arendt opposed them . . . hairsplitting, obtuse**: Hannah Arendt, "Reflections on Little Rock," in Baehr, ed. 231-46.

## Imagine

**war-making was the only compelling thing the governing party could imagine:** Jane Mayer records a revealing transformation in

President Bush, who appeared to find his presidency's purpose only when war became wageable. "'I never felt more comfortable in my life'" he said, once the "war on terror" had been launched. "The president confided that it had given him new purpose. . ." *The Dark Side* (New York: Doubleday, 2008) 48.

**National Priorities Project:** http://www.nationalpriorities.org/cms/tradeoffs.

## Banner Peak

**"I was suddenly brought to a dead stop":** John Muir, *The Mountains of California* (1894: rpt. San Francisco: Sierra Club, 1988) 51-52.

## "Un-Hating the Muir Trail

**"Pat, pat, shuffle shuffle":**  Muir's comment is from a manuscript scrap dated as "probably 1870." Frederick Turner, *John Muir: Rediscovering America.* (New York: Perseus, 1985) 243.

## Red Door

*Hundreds of thousands*: Howard Zinn, "Robber Barons and Rebels" in *History is a Weapon* (http://www.historyisaweapon.com/defcon1/zinnbaron11.html) [n.p.].

**Harrison visited Portland that year and reviewed the Guard:** Harry L. Wells, "The Oregon National Guard," *The Californian Illustrated Magazine* (October 1891 – May 1892) 95-97.

**organized and commanded:** Howard Zinn, "Robber Barons and Rebels" in *History is a Weapon* (http://www.historyisaweapon.com/defcon1/zinnbaron11.html) [n.p.].

**"the only book of its kind":** Michel de Montaigne, "On the affection of fathers for their children" (II.8), *The Essays,* trans. M.A. Screech (London: Penguin, 1987) 149.

## Rendition

**"Over one thousand CIA-operated flights":**  "CIA activities in Europe: European Parliament adopts final report deploring passivity from some Member States." European Parliament. Justice and home affairs. 14 February 2007. http://www.europarl.europa.eu.

**Vice President Cheney foresaw Republican dominance:** Details in Tom Hamburger and Peter Wallsten, *One Party Country: The*

*Republican Plan for Dominance in the 21st Century* (New York: Wiley, 2006).

**The "Project for the New American Century". . . website:** www. newamericancentury.org (*Note: website is since suspended*).

**From London and Dublin . . . hundreds of secret CIA airplanes:** see Stephen Grey, *Ghost Plane: The True Story of the CIA Torture Program* (New York: St. Martins, 2006).

"The Sunday Times of London has obtained evidence that the US government is leasing a special Gulfstream Jet to transport detained suspects to other nations that routinely use torture in their prisons. Logs for the airplane show the Pentagon and CIA have used the plane more than 300 times and dropped off detainees in Syria, Egypt and Uzbekistan." 17 November 2006. http://www.democracynow.org.

According to the EU, at least 147 flights stopped in Irish airports. "CIA activities in Europe: European Parliament adopts final report deploring passivity from some Member States" European Parliament, Justice and home affairs, 14 February 2007. http://www.europarl. europa.eu.

**At least fourteen other nations permitted and facilitated this network:** "The European parliament has approved a damning report on secret CIA flights, condemning member states which colluded in the operations. The UK, Germany and Italy were among 14 states which allowed the US to forcibly remove terror suspects, lawmakers said." "EU endorses damning report on CIA." BBC News 14 February 2007.

**fourteen thousand humans held in US military or CIA prisons:** Patrick Quinn, "US War Prisons Legal Vacuum for 14,000," The Associated Press, 16 September 2006.

**On the morning of 10 March 1948. . . the body of Jan Masaryk:** Jack Messenger and Brigitte Lee, *Globetrotter Travel Guide Prague*, 4th ed. (London: New Holland, 2006) 72.

**One morning during the Argentine dictatorship. . . the journalist Rodolfo Walsh:** Michael McCaughan, *True Crimes: Rodolfo Walsh: The Life and Times of a Radical Intellectual* (London: Latin American Bureau, 2002).

## After Rendition. . . Silence

**Hints and premonitions:** Maher Arar and Khaled el-Masri were both released from extraordinary rendition, detention, and torture in 2003, after which their stories gradually became part of the "nonsecret."

**"one of the biggest nonsecrets in Washington":** "Torture by Proxy." Editorial. *New York Times* 8 March 2005: A22. *Times* coverage began with Douglas Jehl and David Johnston, "Rule Change Lets CIA Freely Send Suspects Abroad," *New York Times* 6 March 2005: 1.1.

**"the eternal and unremitting force of the habeas corpus laws":** Thomas Jefferson. Letter to James Madison 20 December 1787. *Heath Anthology of American Literature*, vol. A. Paul Lauter, ed. (New York: Houghton Mifflin, 2006) 1012.

**An American citizen, taken on American soil:** Jose Padilla, a native-born US citizen, was arrested 8 May 2002 in Chicago and held in a military brig until November of 2005 – incommunicado for the first two years. Shortly before the Supreme Court was expected to rule on challenges to his imprisonment, Attorney General Ashcroft dropped his status as an "enemy combatant" and arranged to try him in criminal court. Eric Lichtblau, "In Legal Shift, US Charges Detainee in Criminal Case," *New York Times* 22 November 2005: A1. Padilla was convicted and sentenced; appeals are pending.

**half-million Iraqis had been killed:** Gilbert Burnham, Riyadh Lafta, Shannon Doocy, Les Roberts, "Mortality after the 2003 invasion of Iraq: a cross-sectional cluster sample survey." *The Lancet* 11 October 2006. The civilian casualty estimate arrived at in this study is 654,965 as of July 2006, or 2.5 percent of the population.

**four million turned into homeless:** the United Nations High Commission on Refugees (UNHCR) estimate of external refugees is over two million as of September 2007, and of "internally displaced persons" 2.3 million. *UNHCR Global Report 2007*: 305-06. http://www.unhcr.org/home/PUBL/484908962.pdf.

**"we cannot tell our people a story that sticks....":** Barry Lopez, *Resistance* (New York: Vintage, 2005) 10.

**"sentence that might break through":** Lopez 21

**a full half of the 2004 electorate:** The Harris Poll of 21 October 2004 found 62 percent believing "that Saddam Hussein had strong links to Al Qaeda." The poller remarks, "More surprising perhaps are the large numbers. . . who believe claims which the president has not made, and which virtually no experts believe to be true: 41 percent believe that Saddam Hussein helped plan and support the hijackers who attacked the U.S. on September 11, 2001. 38 percent believe that Iraq had weapons of mass destruction when the U.S. invaded. 37 percent actually believe that several of the hijackers who attacked the U.S. on September 11 were Iraqis." The Harris Poll #79. http://www. harrisinteractive.com/harris_poll/index.asp?PID=508.

**President, Vice-President, and Secretary of Defense:** "US President George Bush has said there is no evidence that Saddam Hussein was involved in the 11 September attacks. The comments - among his most explicit so far on the issue - come after a recent opinion poll found that nearly 70% of Americans believed the Iraqi leader was personally involved in the attacks. Mr Bush did however repeat his belief that the former Iraqi president had ties to al-Qaeda. . . . Critics of the war on Iraq have accused the US administration of deliberately encouraging public confusion to generate support for military action." "Bush rejects Saddam 9/11 link." BBC News 18 Sept 2003. http://news.bbc.co.uk/2/hi/americas/3118262.stm.

**Cheney** admitted the same during the Vice Presidential debate (though clouded by obfuscating comments to the contrary): "I have not suggested there's a connection between Iraq and 9/11. . ." "The Cheney-Edwards Vice Presidential Debate," 5 October 2004, *Commission on Presidential Debates*. http://www.debates.org/pages/trans2004b.html.

**Rumsfeld** had admitted the fact on the day before Cheney's admission at a 4 October 2004 Council on Foreign Relations conference: "Mr Rumsfeld was asked by a New York audience about connections between Saddam Hussein and Osama Bin Laden. 'To my knowledge, I have not seen any strong, hard evidence that links the two,' he said." (He later backtracked on this admission.) "Rumsfeld questions Saddam-Bin Laden link," BBC News 5 October 2004. http://news.bbc.co.uk/2/hi/americas/3715396.stm

**"entertained at the point of a sword":** Richard Drinnon, *Facing West: The Metaphysics of Indian-Hating and Empire-Building* (New York: Schocken Books, 1980) 42. "Down fell men, women, children" is the laconic conclusion of this officer's account.

**Arthur Miller's comment. . ."We were all going slightly crazy":** qtd. in E.J. Dionne, "Re-Engaging Arthur Miller and Moralism," *Oregonian* 15 February 2005: B9. (This is an oft-repeated quote but its origins are hard to find, perhaps apocryphal.)

**On the fifteenth day of November, 2007, a Congressperson stood in the well:** Rep. Lloyd Doggett of Texas: "This is an Administration that has desecrated our Constitution, debased our values and repeatedly undermined our freedoms. For a party that purports to hate Big Government, these Republicans sure do seem to love Big Brother. They demand unlimited Executive power and unrestrained authority to intrude into our everyday lives. Today, we dare to impose some limitations on one of so many examples of their callous disregard of our liberties. . ." *Congressional Record – House,* H13972.

## And after Silence?

William Butler Yeats translated Swift's Latin epitaph:

> Swift has sailed into his rest;
> Savage indignation there
> Cannot lacerate his breast.
> Imitate him if you dare,
> World-besotted traveller; he
> Served human liberty.

## Lacking the Subjunctive

**"If I was rich . . ."**: in some languages this usage would require a separate verb form called the "conditional." In English, since there's no distinct form for it, the conditional is often categorized as a part of the subjunctive.

**"just a guess"**: "Before, during and after the invasion of Iraq, with a rising sense of alarm, the CIA, the State Department's Bureau of Intelligence and Research (INR), and other agencies warned the Bush-Cheney team that the destruction of Iraq's central government could tumble the country into a civil war. In 2004, of course, the president famously dismissed such CIA warnings as 'just a guess.'" Robert Dreyfuss, "The truth dawns on Bush." Salon.com 10 April 2006. www.salon.com/opinion/feature/2006/04/10/dreyfuss/.

## The Real Fake

**"He was so real"**: citizen quoted by reporter Jeff Wilson, "Mourners pay respects to Reagan," (*Oregonian* 8 June 2004) A1.

**"sexual selection," as Darwin called it**:  Charles Darwin, *On the Origin of Species* Facsimile of First Edition (Cambridge, Mass: Harvard University Press, 1964) 88-90.

**In one of his earlier books**: Stephen Jay Gould, *Ever Since Darwin* (New York: Norton, 1977) 79-90.

"the American imagination demands the real thing": Umberto Eco, *Travels in Hyperreality.* Trans. William Weaver (New York: Harcourt, 1983) 8.

"kitsch reverence": Eco 10.

Apparently, on a bluff: A Rand Corporation cold-war specialist later told a reporter that the large nuclear arsenals really had been mainly for show – "it is . . . better for our own domestic stability *as well as international perceptions* that we remain good competitors even though the objective significance of the competition is. . . dubious" [emphasis added]. Qtd. in Howard Zinn, *A People's History of the United States* (New York: Perennial/HarperCollins, 2003) 584.

## When Denial is Public Policy

two of Exodus International's "ex-gay" co-founders: Michael Bussee and Gary Cooper.

## O Felix Obama

Storytelling . . . a way of connecting our private imaginative lives with the public realm: Hannah Arendt's work develops this idea in many places. See for instance "The Public Realm: The Common" (from *The Human Condition*) in *The Portable Hannah Arendt.* Peter Baehr, ed. (New York: Penguin, 2000) 199-205. A good recent exploration of these ideas is Michael Jackson, *The Politics of Storytelling: Violence, Transgression, and Intersubjectivity* (Copenhagen: Museum Tusculanum Press, 2002).

Frank Kermode's book: *The Sense of an Ending* (New York: Oxford University Press, 1966) 30.

*evangel*: from Greek *eu* + *angelos*, good messenger, according to Webster's New World Dictionary.

## I Am Already Dead

Names have been changed in this essay to respect student privacy.

## Night Thoughts and Music, Three Days before Election

"Politics – so superficial": Thoreau quote is truncated from: "What is called politics is comparatively something so superficial and inhuman, that practically I have never fairly recognized that it concerns me at all." Henry David Thoreau, "Life Without Principle" (1863), in *Walden and Other Writings.* Ed. Brooks Atkinson (New York:

Modern Library, 1950) 730-31.

**"This life of anger and telegrams":** in *E.M. Forster: The Critical Heritage.* Ed. Philip Gardner (London: Routledge, 1997) 124.

**Gandhi:** imprisoned at thirty-nine years old in the Volksrust Jail in 1908 (Transvaal, South Africa), Gandhi found Thoreau's *Civil Disobedience* in the prison library. "A masterly treatise," he said – "It left a big impression on me." Louis Fischer, *The Life of Mahatma Gandhi* (New York: Harper, 1950) 87-88.

**Mandela:** according to his biographer, Nelson Mandela "admired Gandhi as one of the pioneers of South Africa's liberation movement." But Mandela saw nonviolence, in his words, as "a tactic," "not as an inviolable model." Anthony Sampson, *Mandela* (New York: Knopf, 1999) 68.

Breinigsville, PA USA
18 September 2009
224294BV00002B/3/P